Disclaimer

The goal of this book is to give basic information on the vineyards and wineries of New England. Although the authors have exhaustively researched many sources to ensure the accuracy and completeness of the information contained in this book, the publisher and authors assume no responsibility for errors, inaccuracies, omissions or any other inconsistency herein. Any slights against people, organizations or places are unintentional.

Most of the information in Part Two was supplied by the individual wineries and their web pages. The authors have tried to relay all the information and apologize for any errors that may have slipped into that section. Much of the information in that section changes periodically. Please check with the wineries for current selections, prices and services. Availability of some of the wines and products mentioned in this book may be for a limited time or with a limited quantity. It is best to check with the wineries for up to date information. Please remember that the web pages mentioned in this book may, over time, change, move or cease to exist. You may need to call or write for more information.

The photographs in this book are reproduced as historic illustrations to the text. All of these photographs came from either the wineries themselves; Chris and Nancy Obert; Janet Bell; Kelly Colucci; Jeremy Mayhew; or Nova Development Corporation (NDC) software. The clip art came from Nova Development Corporation and Broderbund software. The winery logos were obtained from the wineries or from their marketing material. All of the maps in this book were either supplied by their sponsors or created by the authors using DeLorme "Street Atlas USA 2009 PLUS" software. Most of these images, photographs, logos and maps are copyrighted and are used with permission. Not all of the images are identified. If you are interested in a particular image please contact Pear Tree Publishing and we can give you more information. Any omission or incorrect information should be transmitted to the publisher, so it can be rectified in any future edition of this book. In the event of any question arising as to the use of any material, we regret any inadvertent error and will be pleased to make the appropriate acknowledgments in future printings.

The views and opinions expressed in this book are solely those of the authors (unless otherwise noted) and do not reflect the view or position of the owners of any of the vineyards or wineries which appear, or are referred to, in this book. The views or opinions expressed in the commentary are those of the individuals speaking and do not necessarily represent the views or opinions of the authors or publisher.

The authors and publisher of this book in no way endorse excessive alcohol consumption at home or while visiting the wineries. They recommend the use of a designated driver for the safety of all while visiting the wineries. They also recommend extending your stay to include overnight accommodations to avoid the possibility of impaired driving. The authors and publishers cannot be held accountable for any inappropriate behavior and ask all to act responsibly.

No part of this book may be reproduced in any form or by electronic or mechanical means, including information storage and retrieval systems, without permission in writing from *Pear Tree Publishing*, except in the case of brief quotations used in reviews.

The Next Harvest…

Vineyards & Wineries of New England

By Christopher P. and Nancy S. Obert
Copyright © 2008 by **Pear Tree Publishing**

PEAR
TREE
PUBLISHING

Published by Pear Tree Publishing
An imprint of Obert Publishing, Bradford, Massachusetts
www.PearTreePublishing.net

First Edition

Printed in the United States of America
by Signature Book Printing, Inc., Gaithersburg, Maryland

The Next Harvest… Vineyards & Wineries of New England / by Christopher P. Obert and Nancy S. Obert – 1ˢᵗ Ed.

ISBN 978-0-9749291-8-7
Library of Congress Control Number: 2008933877

1. New England Wine – Authors 2. Wine – New England 3. Vineyards – New England
4. Vacation – New England
I. Title II. Wine III. New England Wine IV New England Vineyards

Book and cover design: by Christopher P. Obert
Front cover top photo (Chardonnay, green grapes) – Kip Kumler, photographer; Turtle Creek Winery
Front cover bottom right photo (wine glasses) – Janet Bell, photographer
Front cover bottom left photo (New England church) – Nova Development Corporation
Back cover top right photo (Cabernet Franc, purple grapes) – Janet Bell, photographer; Sakonnet Vineyards
Back cover top right photo (barrels & tanks) – Blacksmiths Winery
Back cover top right photo (autumn trees) – Nova Development Corporation
Front endsheet photo (Noiret Grapes) - Jeremy Mayhew, photographer; Candia Vineyards
Back endsheet photo (Frontenac Gris Grapes) - Jeremy Mayhew, photographer; Candia Vineyards

Dedication

To our parents: Agnes and Hervé Blanchette and Giovannina and Norman Obert

Our children: Shari and Jason

And Kathleen (Goldrick) Wilson
Forever in our hearts…

Table of Contents

Table of Contents

Part Two:

Acknowledgments

New England (NDC photo)

"Hey Man, I'm drinking wine, eating cheese and catching some rays."
- Donald Sutherland as "Oddball" in *Kelly's Heroes* (1970)

We would like to thank Bob Dabrowski, owner of Candia Vineyards. Bob was extremely helpful throughout the production of this book. He checked some of our wine and grape facts and added useful comments throughout the writing process. He invited us to his winery and gave us one of the best tastings that we have ever had. Not wanting anyone to be left out, he put us in contact with new wineries not yet open. He even volunteered to help us with an idea we had for a follow up New England wine book. He is an excellent wine maker and an even better person. Thank you Bob!

Phil DeNault and Karen Broadhurst

We would like to thank everyone that helped us with the book or gave us their support: Phil DeNault, Karen Broadhurst, Phil Nanzetta (Signature Book Printing, www.Signature-Book.com), Janet Bell (photos), Kelly Colucci (photos), Jeremy Mayhew (photos), Lorraine Charowsky (photo), Mark Frulla, Paul and Delcie Thibault, Trish and Frank Genghini, Gail Dexter (Director of Development, Southern New Hampshire University), Bill Nelson (Wine America, www.wineamerica.org.)

Thanks to all of our family and friends that supported us: Shari Obert, Jason Obert, Ashley Snow, Jason Percival, Norma and Larry Ayers, Geremy Ayers, Norma Obert, Karen Broadhurst, Phil DeNault and his friends Tony, Cindy, Pauline and Ron, Susan DeNault, Laurel DeNault, Mary Marshall, Irene Bodkin, Cheryl and Ken Sweeney, Jim and Jan Davies and their friend Erin, Danny Bowman, Tom Packard, Jerry McConihe, The North Shore Winers (www.Meetup.com), Shawsheen Liquors, Andover, MA, (www.ShawsheenLiquors.com), Bob, Jaime and Avery Fowler; Kurt, Beth and Catherine, and anyone that we may have missed.

We would like to give extra special thanks to: Elena Hovagimian and the Eastern States Exposition - Home of The Big E www.TheBigE.com; Kip Kumler and Tracy Ebbert (Turtle Creek Winery); Manual Morais (Running Brook Vineyards); Anthony and Judith Farraro (Connecticut Valley Winery); Dr. DiGrazia (DiGrazia Vineyards); Christiana Jones (Jones Winery); Maria Miranda (Miranda Vineyard); Linda Auger (Taylor Brooke Winery); Hannah Menzer (Alfalfa Farm Winery); Charlie Caranci (Plymouth Colony Winery); Heather Houle (Flag Hill Winery & Distillery); Dr. Peter Oldak (Jewell Towne Vineyards); Roberta Gerkin (Piscassic Pond Winery); Jim Zanello (Zorvino Vineyards); Sabra Ewing (Flag Hill Farm) and all of the other New England wineries and their staff.

We would also like to thank all of the wineries that sent us labels and press kits: White Silo Farm & Winery; Hopkins Vineyard; Sharpe Hill Vineyard; Turtle Creek Winery; Sakonnet Vineyards; Cantina Bostonia; Alfalfa Farm Winery; Langworthy Farm; Flag Hill Farm; Chester Hill Winery; Truro Vineyards; Candia Vineyards; Piscassic Pond Winery.

We would like to thank everyone that allowed us to use their photos for the cover and endsheets of this book: Kip Kumler (Turtle Creek Winery); Steve Linne (Blacksmiths Winery); Janet Bell and Sakonnet Vineyards; Jeremy Mayhew and Candia Vineyards; and Nova Development Corporation.

We would like to thank the following people and organizations for the use of their maps as illustrations in this book:

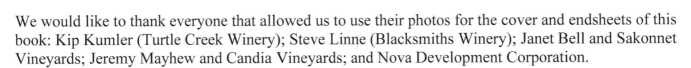

The Connecticut Vineyard and Winery Association and Gary Crump, owner of Priam Vineyards and President of the Wine Council for the use of the Connecticut Wine Trail map. www.ctwine.com

Lisa Capone and the Massachusetts Department of Agricultural Resources for the use of the Massachusetts wine map. www.mass.gov/agr/massgrown/wineries.htm

Stephen Bolpe and the Rhode Island D.E.M. Division of Agriculture for the use of the Rhode Island Wine Trail map. www.RIgrown.gov

Steve Krohn and the The Coastal Winegrowers of Southern New Engalnd www.CoastalWineTrail.com, The Commonwealth of Massachusetts www.MassVacation.com, Newport County Convention & Visitor's Bureau www.gonewport.com, and Southeastern Massachusetts Convention & Visitors Bureau www.bristol-county.org for the use of the Coastal Wine Trail of Southern New England map.

We would also like to thank DeLorme www.DeLorme.com for giving us permission to print their maps in this book.

We would like to thank Steve and Debra Krohn (www.WeTeachWine.com) for offering their assistance with this book. We never got a chance to work with them but we appreciate the offer.

And oh babe, what would you say if we also thanked Hurricane Smith!

We would like to thank all of the wineries, and their contacts, that gave us permission to use material collected from their websites, brochures, wine labels and conversations. If it were not for their openness, friendliness and cooperation, this book would not have been possible!

Connecticut:

Bishop's Orchards Winery - Keith Bishop; Chamard Vineyards - Bridget Riordan; Connecticut Valley Winery - Anthony and Judith Ferraro; DiGrazia Vineyards - Dr. DiGrazia; Gouveia Vineyards - Laura Michnowski; Haight-Brown Vineyard - Tina A. Lambro; Heritage Trail Vineyards - Diane Powell; Hopkins Vineyard - Hilary Criollo; Jerram Winery - Jim Jerram; Jonathan Edwards Winery - Erica Robertson; Jones Winery - Christiana Jones; Land of Nod - William Adam; McLaughlin Vineyards - Frank Carbone; Miranda Vineyard - Maria Miranda; Priam Vineyards - Gloria Priam; Sharpe Hill Vineyard - Steven Vollweiler; Stonington Vineyards - Nick Smith; Strawberry Ridge Vineyards - Rebecca Belarge; Taylor Brooke Winery - Linda Auger; White Silo Farm & Winery - Ralph Gorman

Maine:

Bar Harbor Cellars - Doug Maffucci; Bartlett Maine Estate Winery - Kathe Bartlett; Blacksmiths Winery - Steve Linne; Cellardoor Vineyard - Bettina Doulton; Savage Oakes Vineyard & Winery - Elmer Savage; Shalom Orchard Organic Winery - James Baranski; Sweetgrass Farm Winery & Distillery - Keith Bodine; Tanguay & Son Winery - Daniel Tanguay; Vintner's Cellar Winery - Heidi Shangraw; Winterport Winery - Joan Anderson

Massachusetts:

Alfalfa Farm Winery - Hannah A. Menzer; Broad Hill Vineyards - Michelle Zeamer; Cantina Bostonia - Rodolfo Canale; Cape Cod Cellars - Tim Cooney; Cape Cod Winery - Kristina Lazzari; Chester Hill Winery - Mary Ann Sullivan; Chicama Vineyards - Rosemary Hoeft; Furnace Brook Winery - Deborah Rapp; Hardwick Vineyard & Winery - Jennifer Samek; Les Trois Emme Winery & Vineyard - Wayne Eline; Nantucket Vineyard - Jay Harman; Nashoba Valley Winery - Cindy Pelletier; Neponset Winery - John Comando; Obadiah McIntyre Farm Winery - Nate Benjamin Jr.; Plymouth Bay Winery - Tim Cherry; Plymouth Colony Winery - Charlie Caranci; Plymouth Winery - Linda Shumway; Red Oak Winery - Ann Milmore; Running Brook Vineyards & Winery Inc. - Scott Ellms; Russell Orchards Farm & Winery - Miranda Russell; Truro Vineyards - Kristen Roberts; Turtle Creek Winery - Kip Kumler; West County Cider - Terry Maloney; Westport Rivers Vineyard & Winery - Bill Russell

New Hampshire:

Candia Vineyards - Bob Dabrowski; Farnum Hill Ciders - Louisa Spencer; Flag Hill Winery & Distillery - Heather Houle; Jewell Towne Vineyards - Rich Collins; LaBelle Winery - Amy L. LaBelle; Piscassic Pond Winery - Roberta Gerkin; Zorvino Vineyards - Tom Zack

Rhode Island:

Diamond Hill Vineyards - Peter Berntson; Greenvale Vineyards – Nancy Parker-Wilson; Langworthy Farm Winery - Joe Sharry; Newport Vineyards - John Nunes; Sakonnet Vineyards - Ann Flather

Vermont:

Boyden Valley Winery – Nicholas; Charlotte Village Winery - William Pelkey; Flag Hill Farm - Sabra Ewing; Grand View Winery - Phil Tonks; North River Winery - Annmary T. Block-Reed; Ottauquechee Valley Winery - Annmary T. Block-Reed; Shelburne Vineyard - Kenneth Albert; Snow Farm Vineyard - Harrison Lebowitz

Introduction

New England Wine Labels (Chris Obert photo)

"We could in the United States make as great a variety of wines as are made in Europe,
not exactly of the same kind, but doubtless as good."
- Thomas Jefferson, 1808

How It All Began

Many years ago we began to take long three or four day weekends to explore New England. We would pick either a small out-of-the-way spot or sometimes one of the major cities or tourist destinations. We would stay in a bed & breakfast or a small local motel. Sometimes we would stay at one of the larger hotels. While there, we would visit as many of the local attractions as we could. It was always fun and exciting. It was mostly inexpensive because we would go off season, and that way we could get more for our dollar. On one of these visits we went to a local winery. Unfortunately, we can't remember which winery it was but we had a wonderful time. It was the first time that we had ever visited a winery and also the first time we had ever done a wine tasting. We found it to be very interesting and informative. The hosts were very nice and even though we were not very knowledgeable and did not know much about wine making, they treated us with respect. We were not used to this level of customer service!

We decided to buy a case of their wine and bring it back home. We had so much fun that we started to look for wineries to visit each time we went on one of our weekend vacations. We would buy a case of our favorite wine to bring home and hold us over until our next vacation. Chris, who was not much of a wine drinker before, really liked the chance to try the different wines and started to find wines that he really enjoyed. As time went on he found more and more types of wines that appealed to him. Nancy, who was the wine drinker in the family, found the trips to be a great bargain. She had the chance to try the wines before buying them and the wines were very often sold at a discount, saving her money.

Needless to say, the winery visits became a part of every vacation. Once, when we were planning a family trip to Niagara Falls, we decided to spend part of the vacation in the Finger Lakes Region of New York so that we could try their wines as well. Around this time, our friends and family started to catch on to our adventures, always stopping over after one of our getaways to see what wines we had brought home.

In June of 2007 we were going to visit Rhode Island. Rhode Island was the last of the six New England states where we had not yet visited one of their wineries. Chris decided to see if he could find a book about New England wines before we left on this trip. He found books about European wines and California wines but not New England wines! He looked online and still found nothing. Even when he looked at websites devoted to New England and its wines, the books were all about other locations. We were frustrated because we wanted this trip to be special, and to have gathered a little bit of knowledge about New England wines before we left. That's when Chris said something that would change our lives! He said, "Do you think we could write a book about New England wines?"

You see, Chris owns a small publishing company called Pear Tree Publishing www.PearTreePublishing.net and he is always thinking about books. Chris' company specializes in helping individuals or groups to self-publish their work. He then helps them to market and distribute their book once it is finished. So Chris figured we could turn this trip into a fact finding vacation and started to collect information on the thirty or so New England wineries. Little did we realize that there are over seventy-five vineyards and wineries in New England and that there are many more opening soon!

We decided to give the New England wine book a try. We started to collect as much material from as many sources as possible. We bought a three ring binder and put all of this information together alphabetically by state and then by wineries in each state. By the time we left for vacation we had gathered about thirty pages worth of information.

We visited eight wineries on that first New England wine expedition, three in Rhode Island and five in Massachusetts. As usual, all of the wineries treated us with great care. Who says customer service is dead? It is interesting to note that our normal routine would be to inform the wineries of who we were and that we were doing research for a book only after we had been there for a while. We wanted to see how they acted before they knew that they were being studied. We are proud to say that every winery that we visited treated us the exact same way before they knew about our research and after. They did, however, graciously offer us a lot more information once they knew that we were doing research, which we happily accepted.

This first trip went extremely well and we had such an excited response from the eight wineries that we decided to plan more trips. We ended up making two more large New England wine tours and many smaller missions to discover local wineries. We started to collect vast information and tons of first-hand experiences. We were having a great time.

The only problem that we had was with buying the wines. In the past we would only visit one winery where we would buy an entire case of wine. On this trip, however, we were planning on visiting many wineries, so could not do that. And if things went well, we would be making many more trips. We simply did not have the money to buy that much wine. We did, however, want to buy at least one bottle of wine from each of the wineries and bring it home to share with our friends and family. We did not want nor did we ask for any free wine. We were there for research, not handouts. We decided to buy at least one bottle from each winery and, if we could afford it, more than one bottle. We would ask the wineries about their best sellers or their signature wines and buy those. A problem arose when we liked many of the wines from one winery and bought more than we should have. When we got to the next winery we would have to cut back because we had overspent at the previous winery. By the time we got to the end of each trip we were always running out of money, but we usually spent whatever we had left!

Even on a tight budget, after buying a few bottles of wine from each winery, our wine cellar quickly began to grow. We ended up with nearly ninety bottles of wine over the course of the year we spent doing research. We also ended up with a few dozen wine glasses from the wineries.

With all of this "research" material lying around we just had to host a wine tasting party! Having gone to many tastings, we now wanted to host one ourselves. The event was held in the summer of 2007 and it was a blast. We had so much fun that it led to two more large tastings and over a dozen smaller tastings. At these gatherings we watched, listened and learned. Everyone had their own favorites and everyone had their own comments. It was quite fascinating and informative.

Everything was going great. We had visited many wineries, drank and enjoyed many bottles of wine with our family and friends, and had collected a good amount of information on New England vineyards and wineries. Now all we had to do was put all of this information together in a fun and informative way. We had to make sure our information was as accurate as possible, which was not easy since much of the information changed from year to year. Different grapes are always being tested, wines are made and then sell out, and new wineries are always in the process of opening or, unfortunately, closing.

The first thing that we had to do was contact every New England winery that we could and see if they would agree to become part of a group effort, a group of people and wineries willing to put their rivalries aside and work to put out a book bringing them all together. To our surprise, every winery was in favor of just that, creating a united New England winery group. You see, New York and California have one great advantage over New England. They are each only one state, with one set of rules and laws for each one. New England has six states, each with its own set of rules, laws and middle-men. Each state is working separately, not seeing the big picture. Long before we became involved, the wineries had looked past this and competitors were working together to make New England wine and its wineries better. When we came up with the idea of a wine book they asked us to do whatever we could to help spread the word. New England is making fine wines. New England is an inexpensive and fun vacation destination. And New England vineyards and wineries are here to stay!

So, here we are, two people that have no special background in wine or wine making, writing a book about New England wine. Two people that have, over the course of the last fifteen months, visited dozens of wineries, hosted numerous wine tastings and enjoyed a large selection of fine wines. Now let's see how it all turns out…

Nancy and Christopher Obert (Lorraine Charowsky photo)

Part One

New England

An old Massachusetts burial ground (NDC photo)

"I never drink… wine."
- Bela Lugosi as "Dracula" in *Dracula* (1931)

A Brief History of New England

The landmass of New England was formed hundreds of millions of years ago by a flow of molten rock cooling and becoming what we now call granite. This is highly visible in areas like the quarries of Vermont, the great domed hills like Mount Monadnock in New Hampshire and in the many stone walls early farmers built to mark their property lines. Other geographic upheavals created mountains like the Appalachian range, which begins in Maine and ends in Georgia. During the age of dinosaurs the climate was tropical, so much of New England was inhabited by these dinosaurs. Their footprints can still be seen today at Dinosaur State Park in Rocky Hill, Connecticut. During the Ice Age, when the ice retreated, it created what are called drumlins, one of the most famous being Bunker Hill in Boston, Massachusetts. The terrain of New England was greatly influenced by the geographic events that occurred here millions, and sometimes even billions, of years ago.

North America was first discovered by Leif Ericsson around 1166 on the coast of Newfoundland. It was rediscovered in 1492 by Christopher Columbus who believed that he had reached the West Indies. He landed in what is now called the Bahamas and named the island El Salvador. Over 100 years later the Mayflower voyage of 1620 took permanent settlers to New England. The ship actually landed at what is now called Provincetown, on the tip of Cape Cod. Because the soil was not good for crops, they moved to what became known as Plymouth Colony, which later joined the Massachusetts Bay Colony in 1691. The colonists spread further inland to establish Connecticut in 1639, Rhode Island in 1644, New Hampshire in 1680, Vermont in 1664, and Maine, which was part of Massachusetts until 1820. The origin of the name New England can be traced back to Captain John Smith in 1614, who proudly used the term in reference to the earlier settlement of the land by the English Crown.

Most of the settlers during these early times were small farmers or artisans and lived in small villages. Some looked to the sea for their livelihood, fishing, building ships and trading goods with England and the West Indies. Boston and Newport both became busy ports for the shipping industry during this period. One thing they all had in common was that they insisted on self-government.

The settlers and the Native Americans had a mixed relationship, at times friends and at others times enemies. In addition to the many skirmishes between the Native Americans and the European settlers, some positive outcomes were apparent. Some of these included the knowledge of growing native crops such as corn (known as maize) squash and pumpkins, and the process of making maple syrup from tapping sap from maple trees.

The 1700's became a time of unrest and resistance against British reign for the inhabitants. This was a time of many revolts, including the Boston Tea Party in 1773, the battle at Lexington and Concord and the Battle of Bunker Hill, both in 1775. Although fighting was taking place in all of the colonies, the New England region played a prominent role in the War for Independence.

The War of 1812 slowed down the progress of trade in New England for a short time, but soon after this the textile industry prospered. This began in places like Pawtucket, Rhode Island and spread to other communities as well. Most of these cities were situated along rivers to harness the force of the water to power the mills. New England also became a center for inventions, which is where the term "Yankee ingenuity" was coined. This was a time of immense growth with immigrants streaming into New England to work in the mills and to build roads and railways. Education and literature also became important factors in society during the nineteenth century. There were actually nine colleges founded in America before the Revolution, with four of them started here in New England. The nation's first free library was established in 1833 in Peterborough, New Hampshire.

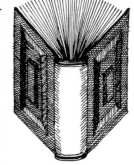

The Twentieth Century saw times of rapid growth due mainly to technical and industrial developments. Textile and shoe mills were prominent throughout the north and east, while paper mills occupied many northern areas. Both World War I and II were booms for industry, but after the wars, industry experienced a rapid decline. The later part of this century did see a rapid increase in technological advancements, especially with the many universities scattered throughout the region, drawing in students from around the world.

Today, New England is using its past to transform its future. Various communities have converted the textile mills into offices and apartments, transformed old homes into historic inns and restaurants, and have used the charm of their scenic towns to draw in visitors. For more detailed information pertaining to New England history, refer to *The Encyclopedia of New England,* edited by Burt Feintuch and David Hatters.

Typical New England coastal scene (NDC photo)

"(Top Producers) really do believe
that their wines reflect the character and personality of an area of land…
and…try hard to express the character of a specific plot in the finished wine."
- Susy Atkins; *International Wine Guide*

A Quick Snapshot of New England

The summers in New England are beautiful, with the weather ranging from warm and sunny days to cool and clear evenings, with a few hotter spells sprinkled throughout the season. Since the region is spread out from mountain ranges in the north to coastal areas along the Atlantic Ocean in the east, the weather can vary greatly, even in a single day. Be prepared with sunglasses and hats or umbrellas, just in case! Summer is the perfect time to explore the many New England farms that offer pick your own berries, including strawberries in June, or blueberries and raspberries in July and August. There is nothing better than homemade strawberry jam or fresh baked blueberry muffins! The amount of recreation is as varied as the landscape. From sailing along the coast to mountain climbing in the White Mountains, New England has a lot to offer.

Autumn is another wonderful time of the year to visit New England since this is when Mother Nature puts on her most spectacular show of color. The foliage season begins in the north as early as mid-August and reaches its peak in the south by mid to late October. When driving along country roads lined with stone walls and over winding hills, the scenery is superb. A quintessential fall activity for most New Englanders is the ritual of apple picking in a local orchard, followed by choosing a pumpkin from the pumpkin patch in anticipation of carving a jack-o-lantern for Halloween! In addition to apples there are other fresh fruits and  vegetables ready to be harvested including grapes. And let's not forget the down home goodness of a New England Thanksgiving dinner.

19

Winter in New England has been described as like wine, "some years are good, some lousy" (Frommer's *New England, 11th edition*, 2002.) Some winters bring large amounts of snow while others bring rain and sleet. Either way, winters here can be pretty cold, but usually turn into magical winter wonderlands. A sleigh ride over snowy meadows or through the woods is a wonderful way to experience the season in typical New England fashion! New England Christmas vacations can be truly legendary with down-hill skiing, snowmobiling or even ice-fishing as favorite activities.

Spring brings the promise of sun-filled summer days, but also brings both rain and mud, which can sometimes last into May. It does bring early blooming flowers, such as crocuses and daffodils, creating a colorful canvas of the land. Spring is a good time to visit New England to witness nature awakening from its winter slumber. Since spring is a time of new beginnings, why not begin your New England adventure with a return to nature visit?

Since the seasons are so varied in New England, it is up to the visitor which season appeals to them the most, but no matter when you visit, there is certainly something for everyone to enjoy. We suggest that you pick up one of the many popular vacation guidebooks to help you plan your New England getaway. For example, Frommer's *New England* (www.Frommers.com) is one of the books we own for organizing our trips within New England. Two books, *The Smithsonian Guides to Natural America - Northern New England* and *Southern New England,* are great guidebooks for nature lovers to help them explore the wild side of New England. Yankee Magazine's publication, *Great Weekend Getaways in New England,* which has "25 driving tours, a perfect day trip for every state, and loads of local secrets" is also worth looking at for more information. For those of you looking for the perfect New England stone wall to photograph, we recommend the book *Good Fences, a Pictorial History of New England's Stone Walls* by William Hubbell.

New England has a lot to offer the vacationing tourist. It is relatively small in size compared to the larger states so many different destinations can be visited in one trip. A New England vacation is similar to a more expensive European vacation. Like Europe, New England has a number of different landscapes, cultures, and activities located relatively close together. Whether visiting a museum in Boston or an antique shop in Vermont, climbing Maine's Mount Katahdin or whale watching off the coast of Nantucket, there is always some place to go and something to do.

The following section is a brief history and overview of each of the New England states, along with a sampling of various activities that we thought were important to these regions. As you travel through the many sections of New England, we encourage you to find your own special corner or favorite place to come back to when you feel the need to remember our country's historic past.

Connecticut

Statehood: January 9, 1788 (5th)
Capital City: Hartford
Population: 3,505,000
Land area: 4,845 sq. mi.; 48th largest
Nickname: Constitution State / Nutmeg State / Provision State
Motto: *Qui transtulit sustinet* (He who transplanted still sustains)
Origin of state's name: Based on the Mohegan word,
Quinnehtukqut, meaning "Beside the Long Tidal River" or "Long River Place."
Website: www.ctvisit.com

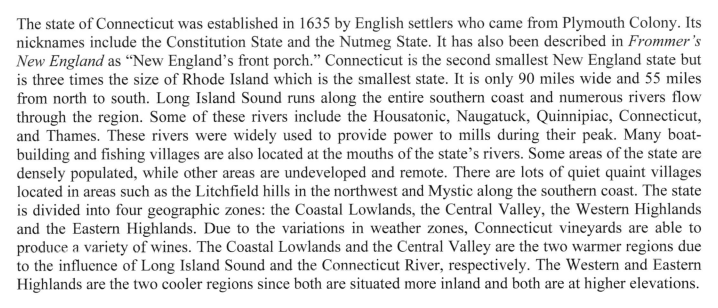

American Robin

The state of Connecticut was established in 1635 by English settlers who came from Plymouth Colony. Its nicknames include the Constitution State and the Nutmeg State. It has also been described in *Frommer's New England* as "New England's front porch." Connecticut is the second smallest New England state but is three times the size of Rhode Island which is the smallest state. It is only 90 miles wide and 55 miles from north to south. Long Island Sound runs along the entire southern coast and numerous rivers flow through the region. Some of these rivers include the Housatonic, Naugatuck, Quinnipiac, Connecticut, and Thames. These rivers were widely used to provide power to mills during their peak. Many boat-building and fishing villages are also located at the mouths of the state's rivers. Some areas of the state are densely populated, while other areas are undeveloped and remote. There are lots of quiet quaint villages located in areas such as the Litchfield hills in the northwest and Mystic along the southern coast. The state is divided into four geographic zones: the Coastal Lowlands, the Central Valley, the Western Highlands and the Eastern Highlands. Due to the variations in weather zones, Connecticut vineyards are able to produce a variety of wines. The Coastal Lowlands and the Central Valley are the two warmer regions due to the influence of Long Island Sound and the Connecticut River, respectively. The Western and Eastern Highlands are the two cooler regions since both are situated more inland and both are at higher elevations.

The Connecticut Winery Act was passed in 1978, which created a rapid growth in the number of wineries opening in the state. Following this Act came the creation of the Connecticut Wine Trail, also in 1978, which is a visitor's guide of driving loops encouraging regional winery visits. There are twenty Connecticut wineries and vineyards covered in Part Two of this book.

Things to do:
In Litchfield County in the northwest corner of the state, you can visit Action Wildlife in Goshen, where you can get an up-close look at three hundred animals on 116 acres of land bordered by classic New England stone walls. Also in this area, be sure to stop at Kent Falls State Park, where you can see the state's highest multi-drop waterfall cascading over limestone and marble.

In Old Mystic, in the southeastern corner, you can visit Clyde's Cider Mill, which is "the oldest steam powered cider mill in the United States" and is a National Historic Landmark.

Along the Thames River in Groton, you can tour the USS *Nautilus*, the world's first nuclear powered ship, at the Submarine Force Museum. Also located in this area are two of the largest attractions in recent years, Connecticut's two casinos, Mohegan Sun in Uncasville and Foxwoods in Ledyard (the largest casino in the United States.)

In the River Valley, located in the center of Connecticut, travelers enjoy visiting towns like Chester and Old Saybrook, both by train and boat. East Haddam is the home of both Gillette Castle and the Goodspeed Opera House, both highlights of a visit to this area.

Maine

Statehood: March 15, 1820 (23rd)
Capital City: Augusta
Population: 1,322,000
Land area: 30,865 sq. mi.; 39th largest
Nickname: Pine Tree State
Motto: *Dirigo* (I direct)
Origin of state's name: Most likely a reference to the region being the mainland, different from its many coastal islands.
Website: www.visitmaine.com

Maine is very large in area, almost as large as the other five New England states combined. There are 3,500 miles of coastline along the state's eastern side, with approximately 3,000 coastal islands, along with millions of acres of undeveloped woodland in the inner regions of the state. The pine and spruce forests found here were extremely beneficial in establishing the lumber trade, making Maine the leading producer of paper products in the United States. The inland area also contains numerous lakes, ponds, rivers and mountains, creating a diverse geographic region. Another important industry in Maine has always been shipbuilding, with Bath being known once as one of the shipbuilding centers of the western world. The most popular tourist regions run from the southern point of the state up the coast to Bar Harbor. Maine is well known for its lobsters, potatoes, moose watching tours and its highest mountain, Mt. Katahdin (5,267 feet.)

The wine industry in Maine is still relatively new, producing mostly fruit wines made with local produce such as blueberries and apples; however, there are a growing number of Maine-grown grape wines also being produced. There are ten Maine wineries and vineyards covered in Part Two of this book.

Things to do:

In the Bar Harbor region a "must" place to visit is Acadia National Park. Located within the park is Cadillac Mountain, which is the highest point (1,530 feet) on the eastern coastline of the Americas, from Canada down to Brazil. Established in 1919, this is also the first national park east of the Mississippi River. There is a twenty mile Loop Road for automobiles that runs through the park, along with numerous carriage paths for biking, hiking trails for all hiking levels, beaches, both rocky and sandy, and wonderful views of the Atlantic Ocean.

The beaches of Maine are also big tourist attractions, with towns such as Old Orchard, Kennebunkport, Ogunquit and York among the most popular places to visit. These coastal towns are filled with restaurants, shops and many different lodging choices, from campgrounds to exquisite inns. Located along the coast of Maine are many historic lighthouses, the most notorious being the Nubble Light located in York. Many encourage visitors to stroll on the grounds, but some are privately owned so check ahead of time for visiting options.

In the woods of Maine you can visit Poland, the home of Poland Springs mineral water, "From Maine, since 1845." On the property is a full service resort, including one of the country's oldest golf courses. Deeper into the Maine woods, hunters still flock to rural areas like Oxbow and nearby Munsungun Lake for incredible hunting and fishing. You can read more about this area and its history in *Bound for Munsungun, the History of the Early Sporting Camps of Northern Maine* by Jack Ahern.

Portland is Maine's largest city but its downtown has the feel of a small town. Walking around among the many small shops is an enjoyable way to spend the day and the city's wide variety of restaurants provides enough choices in cuisine to satisfy any visitor.

Massachusetts

Statehood: May 16, 1788 (6th)
Capital City: Boston
Population: 6,437,000
Land area: 7,838 sq. mi.; 45th largest
Nickname: Bay State / Old Colony State
Motto: *Ense Petit Placidam Sub Libertate quietem*
(By the Sword We Seek Peace, But Peace Only Under Liberty)
Origin of state's name: Named after local Native American tribe whose name means "large hill place."
Website: www.mass-vacation.com

Massachusetts is one of the thirteen original colonies and was the sixth state to ratify the Constitution. Its nicknames are the Bay State or the Old Colony State. The state is loaded with early American history, especially in the areas of Lexington and Concord where the American Revolution began, and in Plymouth where the Mayflower landed. Massachusetts was also known before the Civil War as the literary center of the nation where authors such as John Greenleaf Whittier, Nathaniel Hawthorne, Ralph Waldo Emerson, Henry David Thoreau and Henry Wadsworth Longfellow flourished. Many prestigious colleges are located in the state, including Harvard, MIT, Holy Cross, Boston College and Boston University, where students from around the world flock to every year. The fishing and textile industries have always been a main source of income for many communities, namely in places like Gloucester and in the Lowell/Lawrence area. Massachusetts is well known for fried clams, baked beans and ice cream as local favorites.

Massachusetts has a diverse geographic area, from the Berkshire Mountains in the west to the coastal areas in the east, including Cape Cod and the islands of Martha's Vineyard and Nantucket. This environmental diversity accounts for the wide variety of grapes being grown for wine, along with seasonal fruits like apples and cranberries, which are made into fruit wines. There are twenty-four Massachusetts wineries and vineyards covered in Part Two of this book.

Things to do:
Near downtown Plymouth there is an abundance of New England history to see. You can visit the Mayflower II (a replica of the Mayflower) at the State Pier, along with Plymouth Rock and some of the oldest houses and streets in America. You can also experience life in the 17th century at Plimoth Plantation, a recreation of a 1627 Pilgrim Village.

Boston's Freedom Trail, a three-mile walking tour around Boston, takes visitors to historic places that mainly date back to the American Revolution. From Boston many tourists also flock to Cape Cod and its islands where some of the prettiest beaches in the east can be found.

For the literary buff, there are many historic sites dedicated to local writers, such as Walden Pond, where Thoreau spent much of his writing career, and Whittier's Birthplace in Haverhill, which is still active in keeping the memory of Whittier and his works fresh for future generations. Hawthorne's House of Seven Gables can be found in Salem, which is also the place to be for Halloween, where the town goes all out with festivities celebrating the holiday, including tours of the many witch museums.

In the Berkshire Mountains, you can travel the fifty mile long Mohawk Trail (Route 2) which is one of the oldest roads still in use in the country. The road is an especially pretty way to view the foliage in the fall. Also located in the Berkshires is Tanglewood, the summer home of the Boston Symphony Orchestra.

New Hampshire

Statehood: June 21, 1788 (9th)
Capital City: Concord
Population: 1,315,000
Land area: 8,969 sq. mi.; 44th largest
Nickname: Granite State
Motto: *Live free or die*
Origin of state's name: Named for Hampshire, England, by Captain John Mason
Website: www.visitnh.gov

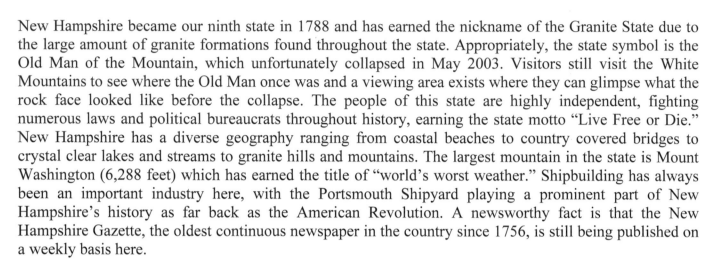

Purple Lilac

New Hampshire became our ninth state in 1788 and has earned the nickname of the Granite State due to the large amount of granite formations found throughout the state. Appropriately, the state symbol is the Old Man of the Mountain, which unfortunately collapsed in May 2003. Visitors still visit the White Mountains to see where the Old Man once was and a viewing area exists where they can glimpse what the rock face looked like before the collapse. The people of this state are highly independent, fighting numerous laws and political bureaucrats throughout history, earning the state motto "Live Free or Die." New Hampshire has a diverse geography ranging from coastal beaches to country covered bridges to crystal clear lakes and streams to granite hills and mountains. The largest mountain in the state is Mount Washington (6,288 feet) which has earned the title of "world's worst weather." Shipbuilding has always been an important industry here, with the Portsmouth Shipyard playing a prominent part of New Hampshire's history as far back as the American Revolution. A newsworthy fact is that the New Hampshire Gazette, the oldest continuous newspaper in the country since 1756, is still being published on a weekly basis here.

New Hampshire's first wineries bottled their first vintages in 1994, making this a fairly new wine-producing state. There are, however, many quality grape wines being made, along with some fruit wines as well. The vineyards and wineries are mostly located in the southeastern corner of the state. There are seven New Hampshire wineries and vineyards covered in Part Two of this book.

Things to do:
The most popular tourist area is certainly the White Mountain region which is a great area to visit in any season. There are many hotels, inns or campgrounds located here and you are within easy driving distance to many tourist attractions, including the Kancamagus Highway and a children's favorite stop, Storyland. The White Mountains are also home to a few of the Grand Hotels that were popular at the turn of the century, including The Balsams at Dixville Notch and The Mount Washington at Bretton Woods.

In Portsmouth there is an outdoor museum called Strawberry Banke, with forty historic buildings open to the public, recreating what this area was like in the early 1630's.

New Hampshire is known for its many covered bridges, which are located throughout the state. The Lake Sunapee region is home to the Cornish-Windsor covered bridge, the longest in the United States.

The Merrimack Valley region includes the cities of Nashua, Manchester and Concord, the state's three largest cities. Here you can find a variety of activities, from the Christa McAuliffe planetarium in Concord to the Robert Frost Farm in Derry.

Rhode Island

Statehood: May 29, 1790 (13th)
Capital City: Providence
Population: 1,068,000
Land area: 1,045 sq. mi.; smallest state
Nickname: The Ocean State / Little Rhody
Motto: *Hope*
Origin of state's name: Possibly named Roode Eylandt by Adriaen Block, a Dutch explorer, because of its red clay or named in honor of the Greek island of Rhodes.
Website: www.visitrhodeisland.com

Rhode Island, the smallest state, became our thirteenth state in 1790. The Atlantic Ocean separates the state into unequal halves and creates numerous inlets, giving the state 400 miles of coastline and various islands within Narragansett Bay. One of the most famous citizens of Rhode Island was Roger Williams, who arrived in 1636 after being exiled from Massachusetts for his religious beliefs. The most popular destination for most visitors is Newport, with its many extravagant mansions open for public viewing. Yachting is a huge draw to the area also.

Rhode Island was producing wine back in the 1600's due to a Charter proclaimed by King Charles II which allowed this, but operation of these wineries ended with Prohibition. The new age of winemaking was reborn in 1975 with the opening of Sakonnet Vineyards in Little Compton. The state is small but it has a large coastline, providing moderate seasons in both summer and winter. This enables Rhode Island to have one of the mildest climates in the eastern United States. There are five Rhode Island wineries and vineyards covered in Part Two of this book.

Things to do:
While in the Newport, RI area, don't miss the Cliff Walk, a three and a half mile walkway overlooking the Atlantic Ocean and running alongside some of Newport's grand mansions. If you have time, we recommend going into some of the mansions and experiencing the majesty of these homes. Many are open to the public, for a fee, and recapture the glamour of the high society of the past.

Located twelve miles off the coast of Rhode Island, and accessible only by boat, is Block Island, a very peaceful and secluded island that draws many tourists to its steep cliffs and natural habitat.

The capitol of Rhode Island, Providence, has many interesting places to visit. These include the Roger Williams Park Zoo, Federal Hill, known as "Little Italy," and Waterplace Park, home of Water Fire, an art event you won't want to miss.

The region known as South County is home to many of Rhode Island's most popular beaches and resort communities, including Narragansett and Watch Hill. In fact, the Reader's Digest book *The Most Scenic Drives in America, 120 Spectacular Road Trips* lists Rhode Island's "South County Coast" as one of the best scenic drives in New England. Beginning in Westerly and ending in Wickford, this route runs parallel to both Block Island Sound and Rhode Island Sound. We highly recommend this lovely drive and suggest that you check out the ten other New England drives mentioned in this book.

Let's talk about two words that we kept coming across: viniculture and viticulture. We were not always sure what these terms meant or how they differed. We knew that agriculture was the science of the cultivation of soil and the science behind farming but we didn't know how "vini" and "viti" fit in. According to our understanding, viniculture is the science and study of the growing of grapes and the methods used to make them into wine. It is more focused on the production of wine but includes the importance of grapes. Viticulture is the study and practice of growing grapes, especially for wine production, with the emphasis on the growing of the grapes knowing that wine will be made from them. To put it another way, viniculture is like the cook in the kitchen. It is very helpful to understand the fresh vegetables but it is more important to know how to use them in a recipe. Viticulture is more like the gardener, who knows that their vegetables are going to be used in wonderful recipes but it is their job to tend the garden.

Harvest Pruning 2003, Hardwick Vineyards (Hardwick photo)

The beginning of all wines, whether they are red or white, begins in the vineyard. We won't go into all of the details of growing grapes but any farmer or part-time gardener can tell you that tending a crop can be hard work. The vineyard manager is responsible for the care and health of the vines. The life cycle of a vineyard is complex and each factor affects the quality and yield of the grape harvest. Everything has to be working together from the trellising system, to the pruning, to proper harvesting. Many factors in a region's climate determine how well wine grapes can be grown. Some of these include the length of the growing season, the severity of the winter months and early frosts, the amount of rain in spring and early summer to sustain the vines, and the amount of drier weather at the end of the growing season from late summer to the fall. It is the job of the vineyard manager to work with the environment and take all necessary steps to ensure the health of the grapes. One of their main roles is to monitor the sugar and acid levels in the grapes throughout the growing season. Grapes are then harvested from the vineyard at their peak ripeness, taking care not to bruise the fruit. Any exposure to oxygen can ruin the taste of the wine and trigger the start of microbes in the grapes, turning the wine into vinegar.

Once the grapes are harvested the wine maker takes over. The skins, stalks and seeds are removed and the grapes are crushed into what is called "must." In the making of red wine, the skins are allowed to remain, since the tannins in the skins add more flavor and color to the wine. After being crushed, the grapes are put into tanks to sleep for anywhere from 12-48 hours in order to extract the flavors and aromas. When making white wines, the juice collected from the first pressing of the grapes is made into wine, which is usually filtered and bottled as soon as possible after fermentation to preserve the freshness. Fermentation of the grapes takes place either in stainless-steel or oak tanks. White wines are placed in sealed containers to avoid oxidation and browning, while reds wines are sometimes allowed to ferment in open tanks with the layer of skins floating on top to protect the must. Here, carbon dioxide is discharged by the natural yeasts in the grapes, providing a cushion against air ruining the wine. It is also at this stage that the winemaker must decide whether to add acid or sugar to the wine. The addition of sugar increases the alcohol content, not the sweetness. White wines can be aged for as little as three months, while red wines are usually aged much longer, up to eighteen months for some.

Before being bottled, some wines are filtered, where sediments are removed and the wine is clarified. Bottling is usually automated and done in a sterile environment, protecting the wine from contaminants. There are many shapes and styles of bottles, each signifying a particular wine. This system was determined by the French and the rest of the wine world has followed their lead. Tall, tapered bottles usually hold dessert wines like Riesling and Gewurztraminer, bottles with sloped shoulders hold wines like Point Noir and Chardonnay, and bottles with long, straight sides and pronounced shoulders hold Merlot, Cabernet Sauvignon and Sauvignon Blanc wines. The color of the bottle also determines the wine it contains. Bottles are tinted to protect the wine from light and damage. Green bottles usually contain red wines, clear, light green, or brown bottles contain white wines, with darker tinted bottles holding wines that need to age longer.

Corks are then placed in the bottles to stop air from entering. The piece of cork expands, creating an airtight seal. Some corks are made out of solid cork oak bark, while others are made out of plastic. Some wines don't have corks, but instead are sealed with a screw, or twist-off, cap. This is another effective way to keep air out of the bottle. Bottles of wine should then be stored on their sides, making sure the corks remain moist, ensuring the bottles are airtight. Some wines should be consumed soon after purchasing them, while others benefit from some bottle aging. As a general rule, white wines should be drunk within six months of purchase and red wines within two years in order to appreciate their flavor. When storing wine, keep the bottles in a cool dark place with some humidity and not too much movement or vibrations, which will mix up any residual sediment.

There are other wines that are produced using different methods of fermentation. One of these is sparkling wine, which uses double fermentation, a process that gives this wine its tiny bubbles. After the first fermentation, the wine is blended and bottled, then a second fermentation takes place. Here, yeasts and sugars are added, the bottles are tilted, twisted and shaken to move the sediment into the neck of the bottle, and the wine is allowed to age from one to three years. Another style of wine is fortified wine, where a neutral grape spirit is added to a wine base, then allowed to mature. Depending on the type of wine, this can be added before, during or even after fermentation takes place. Some of the more well-known fortified wines are Sherry, Port and Madeira. Dessert wines are sweeter wines made from grapes that are picked late in the season. These wines are fortified before the end of fermentation and then are usually aged in wood. The most well known of these wines is Muscat. Lastly, aromatized wines are wines that have been fortified with herbs and spices, making them very aromatic. Vermouth is an example of this type of wine, where the herb called wormwood is added to the wine, creating both red (sweet) or white (dry or sweet) wines.

Turtle Creek Winery Barrel Room (Turtle Creek photo)

Spring growth, Sakonnet Vineyards (Janet Bell photo)

"There is no mystery about terroir…everyplace has one."
- Hugh Johnson, Jancis Robinson; *The World Atlas of Wine*

Two excellent books written about the subject of wine making are Matt Skinner's book *Thirsty Work, Love Wine, Drink Better* and Simon Woods' *Vine to Bottle, How Wine is Made*. If you really want to learn more about making wine we recommend Philip M. Wagner's two books *Grapes into Wine, the Art of Wine Making in America* and *A Wine-Growers Guide, The Wine Appreciation Guild*. These two books are commonplace on the shelves of many New England wineries. An interesting book that we found on terroir was Brian J. Sommers' book *The Geography of Wine, How Landscapes, Cultures, Terroir, and the Weather Make a Good Drop*.

Wine and Climate Change

Back in 1976, California wines took first place over French wines at a blind tasting competition, now known as the "Judgment of Paris." It shocked the world because wine aficionados did not think it was possible for American wine, or any other wine, to beat French wine. The American wines came from the Napa Valley region of California, a thirty mile long valley, which is the state's premier wine growing region. It is a combination of sun, water and soil that makes the Napa Valley so special. Unfortunately, rising global temperatures could threaten the growing climate here, which is the key to Napa Valley's grape growing success.

However, there are other conditions besides temperature that allow the Napa Valley to produce premium grapes. These include both the soil, which is a fertile blend of volcanic and oceanic soils produced by earthquakes, and the geography, which provides dry heat during the day and cool Pacific breezes at night.

The warming weather can alter the growing season of the grapes. According to scientists, the Napa Valley is currently at the "climate quality optimum" of 63 degrees, but it is predicted that Northern California will warm by two to three degrees Fahrenheit in the next fifty years. This will affect the grape quality in two ways. If it is too hot, the grapevines will not produce at all, or they will produce more rapidly, yielding lower quality grapes. Growers will need to decide if they want to begin growing different varieties or relocate to a different region.

This temperature change doesn't only affect California but Europe as well. The slow and steady climb in temperature is starting to affect the wine growing regions of France, Germany and Spain, to name a few. Some vintners in Spain are beginning to plant grapes at higher altitudes in the foothills of the Pyrenees, while in Germany, where they are known for producing cool weather white wines, some growers are

beginning to produce warmer weather red wines. Another region of the world could become the new "king" of wine making. According to *Disappearing Destinations* by Kimberly Lisagor and Heather Hansen, "Places that have been traditionally limited to cooler-climate grapes are branching out and producing better wines than in decades past."

The National Geographic essay "Grape Migration" (October 2007 issue) warns that years from now the world wine map could look very different from the map of today. The article states that many wine grape varieties flourish in a narrow climatic niche and that many traditional wine regions are now near their limit. But what is bad news for one region may be good news for another. If the predictions of scientists are correct, and the rise in temperature stays on course, the wine growing regions of the world will change. Some will move many miles from a warm or hot region up to a moderate to cool region. In the near future another blind tasting could put one of today's cooler wine-growing regions on top.

Serving Wine, Tasting Wine

The most frequently asked questions about wine are how to serve it and how to best pair it with food. We are not going to go into detail about serving wine but we feel the most important thing to remember is

temperature. The proper temperature for serving wine varies but most wines are best served between 39° and 64° Fahrenheit, with 50° being the ideal cellar temperature. Sweet wines and dry whites tend to be served cooler than rosés and light red wines. Full bodied reds tend to be served warmer. If you have any questions about their proper serving temperature, we suggest checking the label, since sometimes it is listed or ask the winemaker or wine steward you are dealing with when purchasing the wine.

As for pairing wines with food, the rules for this have changed over the last few decades and are still changing. Today it is mostly personal preferences that drive the pairing of wine and food, however a few basic rules usually apply. One rule is, bold food calls for bold wine, light food calls for light wine. There are many books available to help you pair food with wine such as: *The Frugal Gourmet Cooks with Wine* by Jeff Smith; *Everyday Dining with Wine, 125 Wonderful Recipes to Match and Enjoy with Wine* by Andrea Immer; *Perfect Pairing, a Master Sommelier's Practical Advice for Partnering Wine with Food* by Evan Goldstein and Joyce Goldstein; and *What to Drink with What you Eat, the Definitive Guide to Pairing Food with Wine, Beer, Spirits, Coffee, Tea – Even Water – Based on Expert Advice from America's Best Sommeliers* by Andrew Dornenburg and Karen Page.

A few of the wine books we have in our library that have helped us with our food pairings are: *Champagne, the Spirit of Celebration* by Sara Slavin and Karl Petzke; *The Wine and Food Lover's Diet, 28 Days of Delicious Weight Loss* by Phillip Tirman, M.D.; *The Wine Club, a Month-by-Month Guide to Learning about Wine with Friends* by Maureen Christian Petrosky; *International Wine Guide, Shortcuts to Success* by Susy Atkins; and *The Everything Wine Book* by Danny May and Andy Sharpe.

There are many other sources of information on wine topics at your disposal such as The American Wine Society (AWS) www.AmericanWineSociety.org whose goal is "Promoting appreciation of wine through education." The AWS has a few regional New England chapters. Another great resource is the New Hampshire State Liquor Store www.FindYourOutlet.com and www.nh.gov/liquor/index.shtml. They print and distribute brochures and information sheets on wine and other spirits. You can pick them up at any of their stores. For example, we recently picked up "How to build a wine collection," "Let the wine tasting begin" and "Pairing wine with food." These sources will not only help you with your wine pairing but also help you with one of the most intimidating stigmas surrounding wine, the dreaded "wine tasting."

Many people have told us that they have never gone to a wine tasting because, due to their lack of wine knowledge, they worry that they will look like a fool in front of their friends. Nothing can be further from the truth. Wine tastings can be a source of great fun and can offer a host of new experiences. It all comes down to one person's ability to communicate which flavors they like and which ones they don't like.

The wine's flavor comes from an interpretation of the senses, mainly taste, smell and touch and, to a lesser extent, sight. The taste of the wine, whether it is sweet, salty, sour, bitter or savory, is detected by the taste buds found on the tongue. Sensors on the tongue detect temperature, among other factors. The mouth and nose work together to process the wine's aroma. The brain then combines all of this information to create a description of the wine's flavor. Sight can also play a role in this description. Just as your eye can be fooled by optical illusions, your mind can be influenced by data supplied by the eye (see the interesting question and answer essay in the July 2008 edition of Scientific American.)

Most people agree that the best way to experience the full flavor of wine is with this three step approach. First, look at the wine. Study its color and clarity. Move the wine around in your glass. Watch how it moves, whether it clings to the glass or not. Second, smell the wine. Put your nose deep into the glass and take a sniff. Swirl the wine around in the glass again and take another sniff. Take your time and let you mind consider the aroma. Lastly, taste the wine. Take a good amount into your mouth. Let it wash over your tongue and cheeks. Take into account how it feels and tastes on your tongue. Now, after a moment, try to describe the sensations. The more you practice this the better you will become. This exercise will help you in two ways. First, it will help you to appreciate wine more by allowing you to recognize slight differences. This will lead to a broader range of wine you may find pleasing. Second, it will help you to verbalize your opinions. This will lead to better communications and allow you to find more wines to your liking. To help you, there are many books on wine tasting and appreciation, as well as classes and

videos. It is easy for the beginner to find more information. The book that we used most often was titled *Wine Tasting* by Michael Broadbent. Additionally, we watched the Millennium Interactive Inc. video *The Secrets of Wine*, which we found at the Haverhill Public Library.

Another clue to help you understand wine is to pay attention to the shape and color of the wine bottle. Many wine growers use the same shaped bottle for certain grape varieties. The bottle's color also gives information on the wine inside. Darker bottles allow less light to enter than clearer bottles, affecting how the wine ages. Some experts even consider the thickness of the glass when purchasing wine. So take notice and don't only glance at the label!

Want to Gain New Wine Knowledge? Read More!

"If you taste without reading, your accumulated knowledge will consist of "I like this" and "I don't like that," without understanding the complex and wonderful reasons why wines taste the way they do."
- Danny May and Andy Sharpe; *The Everything Wine Book*

We are not wine experts but we knew that if we were going to write a book about New England wine and wine in general, we had better educate ourselves. We bought our first books to help us explore and understand the world of wine while shopping at Building #19 www.Building19.com. Building #19 is a New England chain of discount stores that always carries books at a huge discount. Because we were going to publish the book ourselves we needed to keep to a tight budget. The first book that we bought to help us understand the wine world was *I Don't Know Much About Wine... but I Know What I Like* by Simon Woods. Mr. Woods wrote a great book and it was exactly what we were looking for. It was informative and funny, an easy read, but full of useful information. The second book was *Wines & Beers of Old New England* by Sanborn C. Brown. This book was equally entertaining and informative. We never realized how rich the history of New England was with its wines, meads and ciders. We could not have chosen two better books to start our research. But they also started a compulsion! We now wanted to find more books on wine. Our appetite was stimulated and we needed something new to read as we drank our New England wines. But books were not enough. We needed to find books on sale. Our Building #19 experience told us that we didn't have to pay full price for our new venture, a home wine library!

Next, we went to our favorite spot to find books at a discount, Edward R. Hamilton, bookseller, www.EdwardRHamilton.com. Hamilton is a large New England seller of books. They have a vast assortment of books available both from their printed catalog and from their webpage. We picked up a few more books from them. As we finished reading or reviewing the books, we went back from time to time to see if any new wine books were available. We also got a few books from the local library's book sale shelf. Books for a buck, you can't beat that. We don't think that there was a day in the latter half of 2007 that one of us did not have a wine book in our hand. And we got them all on sale. Don't you just love that!

One of the last books that we found on sale was the 2004 book *East Coast Wineries, A Complete Guide from Maine to Virginia* by Carlo DeVito. We finally found a book covering New England wines. It is an excellent book and we don't know if we would have started this project if we had found this book right off the bat, but we were enjoying ourselves and it was too late to turn back now. Mr. DeVito's book was great, but of the 326 pages, only 46 were devoted to New England. We decided that we would try and make our book be as high quality as Mr. DeVito's book but leave out the other East Coast states. We wanted to stay focused on New England and nothing but New England! Over all, we picked up approximately 20 books costing about $100!

We are telling you this because you can do this too. For a small amount of money you can find books that will enhance your wine experience. Now we are not saying that you have to read tons of books to enjoy wine, but reading a few may help you to quickly find which wines you favor or help you to discover different products or methods that will be more to your liking. This little bit of knowledge will help you to communicate your wine preferences when visiting a vineyard or winery on your travels. Your friends may be impressed as well! For these reasons we have included the names of many great reference books and other sources of information throughout our book. We hope you enjoy them.

New England Wine

Cellardoor Winery (Cellardoor photo)

"We believe that grape variety, where those grapes come from, and the grape grower's and wine maker's commitment to quality make a difference to what we experience in the mouth."
- Steven Kolpan, Brian H. Smith and Michael A. Weiss,
The Culinary Institute of America's Exploring Wine

This part of the book is divided into two parts. One is about wine, the other is about grapes. To understand one, you need to understand the other. Since we are not wine or grape experts this section of the book was the most difficult part of the book for us to write. It was an interesting challenge to try and find information on these subjects as they pertained to New England's wines and grapes. Most of the information available is usually devoted to Europe or California wines and grapes. To help us gain a wider range of knowledge concerning these topics, we searched many sources. We found the following three books very useful and informative, as well as enlightening: *Champagne, the Spirit of Celebration* by Sara Slavin and Karl Petzke; *International Wine Guide, Shortcuts to Success* by Susy Atkins; and *Good Wine, the New Basics* by Richard Paul Hinkle. They were not New England oriented, but they were helpful none the less.

In this section of the book we took basic wine and grape facts and then saw how they differed here in New England as opposed to other wine regions. We had some of our facts checked by Bob Dabrowski, owner of Candia Vineyards in New Hampshire, but we take full responsibility for any errors. We think we have most of it right but there is a chance that some things may be inaccurate. Also, please understand that the information in these pages is constantly changing. The types of grapes being grown change over time and new developments may occur in the styles and production of wines. What is true today may not be true tomorrow. If you require a more detailed description of New England wines and grapes, we suggest discussing the topic with the New England wineries and vineyards themselves. They will know better than anyone else. However, this section should still give you some useful information to help you while exploring New England wines!

The Second American Wine Revolution!

"The Paris tasting destroyed the myth of French supremacy
and marked the democratization of the wine world.
It was a watershed in the history of wine."
- Robert M. Parker Jr., 2001

Word is slowing getting out that there is a second wine revolution taking place in America today. This time it is not in California but in New England! New England has long been famous for its clean air, fresh water and excellent soil.

Some of the best farmland in the country is located here, but not very many people outside of New England realize that some of the country's best and most unique wines are being made here. This is strange, since in Viking days New England was referred to as "Vinland."

For the past few decades New England wine makers have been experimenting and refining their techniques, and today those results are starting to receive recognition from around the country and even around the world. Some wineries are importing grapes from California, New York and Europe to create their own inspired versions of fine wines, while others are cultivating their own New England vineyards to create truly 100% New England wines. Grape favorites such as Cabernet Sauvignon, Riesling and Chardonnay, as well as the newer varieties such as Foch, Frontenac, Seyval, and many other cold hardy varieties are grown here.

"Wine is bottled poetry."
- Robert Louis Stevenson

If you are looking for something different, remember that New England is home to more than just vines! New England blueberries are some of the finest in the world and they are also being used to create outstanding wines. And let us not forget the cranberry, another New England classic! New England cranberry wines are starting to appear on Thanksgiving tables across the country. New England orchards are also being tapped to create some of the most exceptional ciders and apple wines available anywhere. Last, but not least, the most ancient of drinks, mead, is currently being created right here using the finest New England honey! The time is right to come and explore New England and taste all of its flavors.

New England scenes (NDC photos)

"If something tastes good to you, then it tastes good, and you are right – period."
- Simon Woods, *I Don't Know Much About Wine… but I Know What I Like*

Basic Information on New England Wines

Reds

Red wines have a broad spectrum of styles and depths ranging from smooth and light or soft and medium, all the way up to rich and full-bodied. The type of grape, objective of the winemaker, yeasts, and even the equipment, all help to determine the style of the wine.

Here in New England, winemakers grow grapes such as Baco Noir, Marechal Foch, Frontenac, Steuben, and Noiret, as well as using blends to make their lighter and medium-bodied red wines. After the grapes are initially crushed, the shorter the skin contact time, the lighter the color of the wine becomes. Not only the color is affected but the tannins and heaviness of the wine is also determined by how much skin contact time is allowed. Some New England winemakers have made full-bodied wines from these grapes that have won international acclaim.

Cabernet Franc can be blended with other red grapes such as Merlot and Cabernet Sauvignon, and even with some of the more interesting cold-hardy varieties such as Noiret, St.Croix, and Corot Noir, or can be made as a single varietal by itself. These wines are very earthy, with aromas of raspberries, violets, currants and herbs.

Red Wine (J. Bell photos)

Full-bodied red wines are rich and hearty, have higher tannin levels, and flavors that linger in your mouth after drinking them. Some of the most popular of these wines are Cabernet Sauvignon, Chambourcin, and Cabernet Franc. Cabernet Sauvignon is the most well-known black grape variety around the world, making wines that are firm, with deep aromas of blackberry, cassis, plum and even leather. Because of the high tannin levels, this wine is best when aged for a while, usually in oak barrels. Some New England wineries have had great success blending in their cold-hardy grapes for very interesting Cabernet wines. The winemaker's most important role is to use his skills in aging and blending to make the most approachable wines, and it is yet another reason to explore the unique vision that New England winemakers offer their guests.

Meritage

There are three famous grapes that when blended together create a fine wine known as a *Meritage*. This mix is widely known and used throughout California. These three grapes are Cabernet Franc, Cabernet Sauvignon and Merlot. All three grapes create hearty red wines that when blended together bring out each other's best qualities, while taming some of their unpleasant qualities, such as the high tannin levels in Cabernet Sauvignon. All have similar aromas and all go well with cheese and hearty foods like grilled meats and pasta with red sauce. Today all three of these grapes are grown in New England, each of them used to create New England's own version of Meritage.

The reason that we are mentioning Meritage is because New England wine makers are creating fine wines in a similar manner to California winemakers. Here in New England, the winemakers are blending our cold-hardy grapes to create our own style of blends, which are exciting and new, fresh, vibrant tastes to explore.

Whites

White wines can range in style and flavor from dry and light to fruity and spicy and even go up to rich and oaky. White wines are usually served chilled.

Starting with dry and light wines, there are Riesling, Muscadet and Pinot Grigio as some examples. Riesling wines are known for their aromatic fruitiness with a clean, crisp finish, just as our locally made wines from the Cayuga grape. There are wonderful aromas of peaches, apricots, apples and citrus. They are versatile wines sometimes served as an aperitif, but can also be served with spicy foods. There are many dry white wines in New England, including Seyval, LaCrosse, Chardonnay, Pinot Grigio, and Vignoles and these too can be made in styles ranging from lighter to heavier, and drier to sweeter. Here in New England, we have cold-hardy varieties such as Vidal, Valvin Muscat, and LaCrescent that make wonderful off-dry wines, often with amazing aromas of the more famous Muscat wines.

Rosés

Rosés are wines that are typically made by removing the fresh crushed grapes from the skins quickly, allowing very little contact time for the juice to take color from the skins. Red wine can be blended with white wines to give a pink color to the resulting wine. Most people enjoy drinking a rosé chilled while nibbling on a cheese platter outside on a patio on a warm summer day. The best time to enjoy a rosé is while the wine is still young and fresh, as these wines are not meant for aging like a full-bodied red wine. There are many grapes that can be used to make rosé, including Cabernet Franc, Merlot, Seyval, Foch, Chambourcin, Chancellor and Chelois.

Polar Bear Gang

There are three varieties of grapes currently being grown in New England that were all developed by the University of Minnesota in 1995 and are referred to as the "Polar Bear Gang," a name given to them due

to their cold-hardiness and resistance to disease. They can tolerate frigid northern winters, often tolerating temperatures below zero degrees Fahrenheit. These grapes are Frontenac, LaCrescent and St. Pepin.

Frontenac produces red wines that are deeply colored and moderately low in tannins, with pleasing aromas of cherry, plum and berries. LaCrescent and St. Pepin both produce white wines that are fruity and fairly sweet. LaCrescent wines have fantastic aromas and spectacular flavors. St. Pepin wines are similar to either Riesling or Muscat in both style and taste.

There are many more varieties of grapes in the gang, including Bluebell and Edelweiss, and it is quite possible more of these grapes will find their way to New England. So, the next time you are visiting New England don't forget to check out their Polar Bear wines.

Dessert

Sweeter dessert wines tend to be a deeper golden color than white wines and have a thicker texture as well. The aromas are usually very strong and pronounced with scents of apricots, lemons, honey or toffee. These wines are meant to be enjoyed with dessert or as a dessert by themselves. Some of the grapes commonly used to make dessert wines are Gewurztraminer, Muscat and Riesling. Most of these wines get their sweetness from allowing the grapes to ripen longer on the vines, sometimes even freezing on the vines, producing what are called "ice wines." Some grapes are also allowed to become acted upon by botrytis rot, which removes the water from the grapes, allowing the sugars to become concentrated, producing a wonderfully sweet and aromatic dessert wine.

Dessert Wine,
No Longer Just for After Dinner!

New England has followed the lead of New York State and Canada and has begun to create some outstanding dessert wines. These sweeter wines can be made from the same grape varietals that grow well in the shorter New England growing season. The wineries, using these varietals and their own personal techniques, are creating diverse types of sweet wines, dessert wines and ice wines, all boasting of their own flavor and tradition.

The world of dessert wines is undergoing an exciting change. No longer solely served after dinner, the new dessert wines are now being enjoyed before dinner, during dinner, or believe it or not, during breakfast and even at tea-time.

These sweet wines, usually served chilled, are now starting to appear in finer restaurants as an aperitif, an alcoholic beverage served as an appetizer. The role of the aperitif is to quicken the pulse and create anticipation for the coming meal. These wines are also being served during the meal. The usual rule of thumb for pairing wine with food is that strong hearty foods go well with strong hearty wines, while light foods usually go well with light wines. The thought behind this rule is simple you don't want one to overpower the other. But clever chefs are realizing that just as cool and light celery and Blue Cheese dressing can complement hot and spicy Buffalo wings, cool and sweet dessert wines can complement certain spicy foods. So, the next time you are out at a restaurant that is serving spicy foods, don't be surprised if they recommend a sweet New England wine to accompany your meal!

These delectable wines are also starting to appear during the day at some of the finer outdoor cafés. A cool sweet ice wine enjoyed during a hot summer afternoon can be a refreshing treat to savor with your loved one! Or maybe you would like to try these heavenly wines shared as a morning treat served slightly warmed, over a bowl of chilled fresh passion fruit. The adventures you could share enjoying these fine New England wines are as wide as your imagination!

Running Brook Vineyards & Winery 2005 Frost Wine and Boyden Valley Winery's Ice Wine

Chardonnay

Chardonnay, a *vinifera*, sometimes known as the King of White Grapes, is by far the most popular white grape variety. In 1999, it was determined that Chardonnay is one of the possible sixteen descendents from the ancestral Pinot and Gouais Blanc crossing. It is easy to grow, disease resistant and grows well in most conditions. Chardonnay is one of the three grapes used in the making of Champagne. Its flavors can range from dry and light to medium and full-bodied depending on the aging process used. Some wines made are considered big and buttery; others are described as rich and oaky, while still others are unoaked and are closer to Chablis in style. The flavors of the fruit tend to be crisp and fruity like apples, pears and lemons, but can also lean towards oak, butter and vanilla. Chardonnay has been called "The white variety of the last twenty years" (Robert Joseph - *The Wines of the Americas*). Chardonnay should be served between 50-55° F and goes best with lighter foods such as pork, poultry, shellfish, pasta with white sauce and salads.

Running Brook Vineyards, Sakonnet Vineyards, Greenvale Vineyards, Westport Rivers Vineyard, Turtle Creek Winery, Heritage Trail Vineyards, Hopkins Vineyard, Jonathan Edwards Winery, Land of Nod, McLaughlin Vineyards, Sharpe Hill Vineyard, Broad Hill Vineyards, Stonington Vineyards, Strawberry Ridge Vineyards

Chardonnay, ENTAV clone 95, Turtle Creek Winery (Kip Kumler photo)

Chelois

Chelois, pronounced either "shell-oy" or "shell-wah," is a French-American Seibel that is popular in the Eastern and Midwestern United States. It is very often blended with other red grapes to produce blends and rosés with a hint of Burgundy. Chelois grows well in cooler climates, buds late and ripens early and is sometimes described as grassy-tasting. It is prone to fungal disease, vulnerable to bunch rot, and requires cluster thinning. Vineyards that decide to grow this tasty variety show extra dedication to the grape. The results are well worth the effort as Chelois ages gracefully and produce a wonderful tasting wine.
Broad Hill Vineyards

Chelois Grapes, Broad Hill Vineyards (Broad Hill photo)

Concord

Concord was introduced to the Northeastern United States sometime around 1850 by Ephraim Bull. It is a hardy Native American *vitus labrusca* variety which produces delicious grape juice. Welch's started producing its juice in 1869 and is still extremely popular today. Concord grape juice is known for its taste as well as its health benefits. The grapes contain flavonoids, which are powerful antioxidants that help to improve circulation and contribute to healthy blood pressure. Concord is also used to make grape jelly, which typical Americans grew up with in their "PB&J" sandwiches as children. Some Concord is used to make sweet wine, such as kosher wine. It is also used in sherries and ports.
Grown throughout New England

Concord Grapes (Chris Obert photo)

Diamond

Diamond is an American native and hybrid grape created in the late 1800's in Brighton, NY by Jacob Moore. Moore crossed the Iona, a *vinifera-labrusca* hybrid, with Concord to produce a white grape with some traditional Concord aromas. It is still widely grown in western New York and is used to create sparkling blends and off-dry white wines. It is also very popular as a table grape.
Candia Vineyards

Dornfelder

Dornfelder is grown mostly in Germany and was created in 1955 in the town of Weinsberg by crossing the Helfensteiner and Heroldrebe varieties. It is considered the most successful red wine crossing in the history of Germany. Dornfelder produces a light, smooth red wine with hints of blackberry, strawberry and cherry aromas, is low in tannins, and is best served lightly chilled.
Sharpe Hill Vineyard

Frontenac

Frontenac is a newer French-American hybrid released by the University of Minnesota in 1995. It is a cross of Landot 4511 and Native American *vitis ripara*. It is a vigorous cold-hardy variety that is also disease resistant. Frontenac produces high quality, full-bodied red wines that are deeply colored and are moderate to low in tannins. It blends well with other low acid red wines such as Leon Millot. There are very pleasing aromas of cherry, plum and berries.
Candia Vineyards, Connecticut Valley Winery, Savage Oakes Vineyard

Frontenac, Candia Vineyards (Bob Dabrowski photo)

50

Gamay (Gamay Noir)

Gamay, a *vinifera*, originated in Burgundy and is still one of the top ten most planted red varieties in France. It also thrives in Ontario, Canada, but outside of France, most grapes are not a true Gamay, but are actually a clone of Pinot Noir! In France it is used to make Beaujolais, which is a light, fruity red wine, and accounts for half of all the wine produced there. There are also different varieties being grown in California. Gamay is very fruity, light pink to purple in color, low in acidity, has soft tannins and is usually served slightly chilled.

Sharpe Hill Vineyard

Gewürztraminer

Gewürztraminer, a *vinifera*, is most often associated with the Alsace region of France, but its origins almost certainly go back to Italy. The prefix gewürz means "spice" in German. It is the red-skinned form of the Traminer grape, which is prone to vine damage in winter and is a very distinctive grape, highly aromatic with crisp and spicy flavors such as clove and nutmeg, along with vanilla, grapefruit and honeysuckle. The small grapes range in color from pink to bluish-brown and are sometimes made into a "botrytized" late harvest dessert wine. The wines produced have a high alcohol content, usually over thirteen percent. Gewürztraminer is highly aromatic with a strong floral aroma.  It produces full to medium-bodied, medium-dry whites and sweet to very sweet wines and is sometimes described as similar in style to a Riesling. Gewürztraminer is best served at 50-55° F and goes well with Indian curry dishes, pork, and spicy Asian foods.

Sakonnet Vineyards, Newport Vineyard, Priam Vineyards

Labrusca

Vitis Labrusca (Fox Grape) refers to an entire species of grape. Labrusca is a Native American (table) grape grown primarily on the East Coast, with production concentrated in the Lake Erie and Finger Lakes Regions of New York. It has a characteristic "grapey" flavor and is primarily used in products such as juices and jams and includes varieties such as Concord (purple) and Niagara (white.) In America, Labrusca is synonymous with "grape" flavor and is truly an American flavor, not known widely throughout the world.

Grown throughout New England

LaCrescent

LaCrescent is a St. Pepin cross and has lineage dating back to the ancient Muscat Hamburg. It has been included in a group known as the Polar Bear Gang since it is able to survive temperatures below 36° F. This spectacular tasting grape is primarily used in making off-dry or sweet white wines with exotic aromas.

Shelburne Vineyard, Boyden Valley Winery, Candia Vineyards

Landot Noir

Landot Noir is a French-American hybrid and a parent of Frontenac. It is moderately cold-hardy and grows well in the middle-latitude regions of the United States. Landot Noir is primarily used to make red wines with mild intensity that age well. This grape has excellent possibilities in many New England areas.

Sharpe Hill Vineyard, Jewell Towne Vineyards

Léon Millot (Millot)

Léon Millot is the offspring of a North American *Riparia-rupestris* and *Vinifera* (Goldriesling) and is also a cousin of Marechel Foch. It ripens early in a short growing season, which makes it important to the wineries along the Atlantic seaboard. Leon Millot produces structured red wines which are rich in color with well-rounded tannins that can sometimes develop a chocolaty quality with age. In the early part of the 20th century it was used to deepen the paler color of Pinot Noir.
Snow Farm Vineyard, Savage Oakes Vineyard

Malbec

Malbec is mainly grown in Argentina and enjoys the hot summer temperatures. It has also been grown extensively in France where it was used to make rustic wines. The grape is usually left hanging late into the growing season both to let the grape ripen and to soften out the tannins. This produces a wine high in alcohol content, with a deep color and a concentrated juicy dark fruit flavor. It is also occasionally blended with Cabernet Sauvignon to produce a Bordeaux-style blend. It is considered a "big wine" with some taste of plums and spice.
Land of Nod

Marechal Foch

Marechal Foch is the most widely grown French-American hybrid and was developed by Eugene Kuhlmann from a North American *Riparia-rupestris* and a *Vinifera*. It is grown widely in the eastern United States and Canada due to its cold-climate hardiness. It is an early ripening grape that is also vigorous. Marechal Foch makes a light to medium wine with a deep purple color and dark berry flavors. Some describe it as a Beaujolais-style wine, while others compare it to a Pinot Noir.
Flag Hill Winery, Savage Oakes Vineyard, Broad Hill Vineyards

Marquette

Marquette was developed by the University of Minnesota and was introduced in 2006. It is a cold-hardy grape that is frost resistant to minus 36° F. It produces wines that are ruby red in color with fruit and spice flavors that are very pleasant. Marquette is grown mainly in the upper Midwest and Northeastern states.
Shelburne Vineyard, Candia Vineyards

Melon de Bourgogne

Melon de Bourgogne has small to medium grape clusters, is yellow in color and has high tannins in its skin. It was widely grown in Burgundy, in the Loire region of France and is used to make Muscadet. In the United States, Melon makes white wines that are slightly tart and acidic with citrus fruit flavors, making it a great companion to seafood. Because of its sensitivity to frost, it can only be found in limited quantities in the cooler climate of the Northern states.
Sharpe Hill Vineyard

Merlot

Merlot is the most produced grape in the Bourdeaux region of France. It is similar to Cabernet Sauvignon, with which it is frequently blended, but has softer tannins. It has been described as "the red grape of the 1990's – or the next century?" (Robert Joseph - *The Wines of the Americas*.) It is used in California to make a blend of wines called Meritage. Merlot is a mid-season ripening grape that is tolerant of cooler climates, producing wines with flavors ranging from plums and black berries to chocolate and leather.

Running Brook Vineyards, Cape Cod Winery, Haight-Brown Vineyard, Heritage Trail Vineyards, Jones Winery, Priam Vineyards, Taylor Brooke Winery

Muscat (Muscat Blanc)

Muscat is believed to have been one of the first varieties of grapes to be identified and cultivated and every noble grape is believed to be able to trace its lineage back to the Muscat. It has been growing in the Mediterranean region for centuries. Muscat is primarily used in the Northern hemisphere to make semi-sweet and sweet dessert wines with a distinctive aroma and grapey flavor. It has small round grapes that are picked late to maximize their sweetness. The aromas range from apples and pears to coffee and roses. These are the grapes used to make Italy's Asti Spumante.

Priam Vineyards, Jewell Towne Vineyards

Niagara

Niagara was developed in 1868 when C.L. Hoag and B.W. Clark cross-bred the Concord grape with the White Cassady grape in Niagara County, New York. It was introduced commercially in 1882. Originally, the entire grape stock was owned by the Niagara Grape Company and was widely advertised. It is now used as a base for Champagnes, cream Sherries and white grape juice. Niagara is well-noted for its showy appearance, pleasant aroma and strong grapey flavor, which is most likely why it is so popular in Welch's White Grape Juice. It is the top American green grape, just as the Concord, its cousin, is the top purple variety.

Flag Hill Winery

Niagara Grapes, Flag Hill Winery (Flag Hill photo)

Noiret

Noiret, pronounced "nwahr-ay," is a moderately cold-hardy grape that grows in conical shaped bunches. It was created from a complex cross in 1973 in Geneva, New York and was known as NY73.0136. It grows well in the Northeastern United States and is able to withstand temperatures to -14° F. Noiret produces wines with a deep red color, good tannins and unusually robust pepper overtones. NY 73.0136.17 was renamed Noiret in 2006.
Candia Vineyards

Noiret Grapes, Candia Vineyards (Jeremy Mayhew photo)

Pinot Gris / Pinot Grigio

Pinot Gris is a pink-skinned natural mutation of the Pinot Noir grape. It is considered a noble grape and is a cousin of Chardonnay. When grown in Italy it is known as Pinot Grigio. The name translates in French as "gray pinecone," getting the term from the coppery gray grapes it produces. It is grown in cooler climates all over the world and produces conical shaped grape bunches that have intense aromas such as honey and wildflowers. The wines it produces are light to medium-bodied and are dry to medium-dry. They are best served at 45-55° F and go well with all types of food, including light fish, shellfish and pasta with white sauce. According to some, "Pinot Grigio…is the Italian expression – light, delicate, and fresh," and "Pinot Gris…is the French expression – fatter and richer." (*Thirsty Work* by Matt Skinner).
Running Brook Vineyards, Greenvale Vineyards, Jones Winery, Broad Hill Vineyards; Cape Cod Winery

Pinot Meunier

Pinot Meunier is the cousin of both Pinot Noir and Chardonnay and can trace its heritage to northern France. It is the most planted grape variety in the Champagne region. In fact, Pinot Meunier is "the magical third party alongside Chardonnay and Pinot Noir in the Champagne ménage à trois!" (*Thirsty Work* by Matt Skinner). It is a cool climate variety and can be found growing abundantly in the Finger Lakes region of New York. Pinot Meunier produces a wine that is light red to rosé with crisp acidity, sometimes with some smokiness. The wine is usually not allowed to age long, but is best enjoyed young.
Westport Rivers Vineyard

Pinot Noir

Pinot Noir, a *vinifera*, is most famous for making Burgundy wine and is also one of the three grapes used to make Champagne. It is an early ripener and a thin-skinned grape. It usually grows best in cool, foggy climates but is a very difficult variety to grow. It has been called "The 'Holy Grail' for most red wine makers" (Robert Joseph - *The Wines of the Americas*) and is usually referred to as one of the world's noblest of grapes. Flavors can range from red berries and cherries and, as the wine ages, even earthy aromas such as game and mushrooms can be detected. The wine's color is a lighter red than the reds produced in the Bourdeaux region. It is best served at around 55-65° F and complements veal, pork and meaty fish.

Running Brook Vineyards, Snow Farm Vineyard, Sakonnet Vineyards, Diamond Hill Vineyards, Westport Rivers Vineyard, Turtle Creek Winery, Hopkins Vineyard, Land of Nod, Broad Hill Vineyards

Riesling

Riesling, a *vinifera*, is considered to be a "noble" grape that was originally grown in the Rhine region of Germany. In Germany, the grapes produce a semi-dry wine with some sugar content, whereas in the United States the wine produced is a more flowery, fruity wine that is high in acidity and low in alcohol. Colors can range from pale straw to deep gold. The grape grows well in cool climates, but adapts well to most growing conditions and is found in almost every wine-growing state. If the grapes are allowed to be acted upon with botrytis, they can produce wonderful late-harvest dessert wines. In addition, if left on the vine into the winter, the grapes produce outstanding "ice wines" from the frozen grapes. Riesling's characteristics have been described as "...mouth wateringly delicate flavors of fresh ripe peaches, apricots, and melons, sometimes pierced with a vibrant mineral quality, like the taste of water running

over stones in a mountain stream" (*The Wine Bible*). Riesling is best served at 50-55° F and goes well with cheese, smoked fish and spicy Asian and Indian foods. It also goes well with most desserts.

Shelburne Vineyard, Boyden Valley Winery, Jewell Towne Vineyards, Flag Hill Winery, Heritage Trail Vineyards, Priam Vineyards, Savage Oakes Vineyard, Broad Hill Vineyards

Rkatsiteli

Rkatsiteli gets its origin from Eastern Europe, specifically the Caucasus Mountains in Georgia. It is an ancient grape that produces spicy, floral wines similar to Gewürztraminer and Riesling. It grows well in cooler climates such as New York's Finger Lakes as well as in Virginia, New Jersey and Massachusetts.

Westport Rivers Vineyard

Wine Casks, Sakonnet Vineyards (Janet Bell photo)

Seyval Blanc

Seyval Blanc was the first successful French-American hybrid, developed by Seyve-Villard around 1920. It grows in conical shaped bunches and grows well in cool climates in North America and Europe, producing crisp, dry, fruity wines that sometimes resemble a French "Chablis." Seyval Blanc is also one of the parents of Chardonnel and Chardonnay. It is the "most widely grown white hybrid," (The Wines of Americas) and can be made into a delightful variety of wines ranging from light and spritzy, sweet, late-harvest dessert, or even sparkling wines!

Broad Hill Vineyards, Cape Cod Winery, Snow Farm Vineyard, Grand View Winery, Boyden Valley Winery, Flag Hill Winery, DiGrazia Vineyards, Haight-Brown Vineyard, Hopkins Vineyard, McLaughlin Vineyards, Savage Oakes Vineyard, Alfalfa Farm Winery

Seyval Grapes, Alfalfa Farm Winery (Alfalfa photo)

St. Croix

St. Croix, developed by Elmer Swenson, is a cold-hardy grape that grows well in Northern and Midwestern States. It is used for wine, juice, and also as a table grape. St. Croix produces a red wine that is fruity, low in tannins and low in acidity.

Shelburne Vineyard, Priam Vineyards, Sharpe Hill Vineyard, Taylor Brooke Winery, Savage Oakes Vineyard

St. Croix Grapes, Priam Vineyard (Priam photo)

56

St. Pepin

St. Pepin is a close sibling of the La Crosse variety of grape. It ripens early and produces a fruity white wine that some believe is similar to Riesling and Muscat. St. Pepin is cold-hardy so it grows well in the Northern States.

Taylor Brooke Winery, Savage Oakes Vineyard

Traminette

Traminette is a cross between Gewürztraminer and Seyval Blanc and was released in 1996 in Geneva, New York. Traminette grows well in cool climates, ripening mid-season. It produces wines with fresh fruit aromas and flavors that are floral and spicy in both dry and sweet versions. When aged, the wine tastes like honey and apricot.

Shelburne Vineyard, Jewell Towne Vineyards, Taylor Brooke Winery

Vidal Blanc

Vidal Blanc is a French-American hybrid developed by Albert Seible by crossing Ugni Blanc (also known as St. Emilion) with Rayon d'Or. It is a very productive and disease-resistant grape that grows in "winged" bunches. The wine can be fruity and floral in character. Some wineries produce several styles, both with or without oak. Vidal Blanc can produce a variety of styles of wine from dry to sweet, including dessert and ice wines, to sparkling wines. It is well suited to cold climates, which is why in Canada it has been a superior producer of ice wines, where it has been referred to as "the Nectar of the North!"

Running Brook Vineyards, Cape Cod Winery, Snow Farm Vineyard, Shelburne Vineyard, Sakonnet Vineyards, Greenvale Vineyards, DiGrazia Vineyards, Hopkins Vineyard, Stonington Vineyards

Vignoles

Vignoles is a French-American Seibel and Pinot Noir cross that grows well in the cooler regions of the Northeast U.S. and Canada. It produces small, compact clusters of grapes that can be susceptible to botrytis rot when grown in humid climates. It is a late-ripener, usually ripening in late September, producing dry white, dessert and ice wines. Vignoles is high in both sugar and acid, and is fruity and balanced.

Snow Farm Vineyard, Shelburne Vineyard, Heritage Trail Vineyards, Sharpe Hill Vineyard, Taylor Brooke Winery

Villard Noir

Villard Noir is a French-American hybrid that grows well in both cold and warm climates. It is easy to grow and exceptionally productive. Villard Noir is a cross between two Seibel varieties, Le Subereux and Chancellor. It was planted widely in France until 1977. Villard Noir produces wines that are light-bodied and fruity, low in tannins and are commonly used as a blending grape in table wines.

Heritage Trail Vineyards

Zweigelt

Zweigelt is a cross of St. Laurent and Blaufrankisch and was developed in Austria, where it is widely grown. In fact, it is the most popular dark-skinned grape grown in Austria. It is one of the most cold-hardy grapes grown, creating wines that age well.

Shelburne Vineyard

"Grape varieties are all-important.
They have to suit the soil, the climate, and the economy of the region."
- Michael Broadbent, *Wine Tasting*

Frontenac Gris, Candia Vineyards (Jeremy Mayhew photo)

Other New England Choices

New England offers many choices (Chris Obert photo)

"It is the winemaker's skill that turns excellent fruit into fine wine."
- Ernie Loosen (German Winemaker)

As we said in the beginning of the book, New England is rediscovering its beverage heritage. In the introduction we mentioned a book called *Wines & Beers of Old New England, a How-to-Do-It History* by Sanborn C Brown. If you are interested in the history of wines, beers, meads and ciders, we highly recommend his book since it covers much more information than we do. You never know, you may impress your friends with the variety of interesting facts that you can learn while reading his book. Another great book on the often odd varieties of wine is *How to make Table Wine, Country Wine and Beer*, edited by Alison Louw. Her book may be harder to find but it is worth the search. The book gives

detailed information on making wine and provides dozens of interesting recipes, including Barley and Raisin Wine, Beetroot Wine, and Birch Sap and Pear Wine. And those are only a few from the "B's". Alison's book shows remarkable examples of the flavors out there just waiting to be rediscovered. It made us wonder what other beverages and flavors were out there for us to try.

"The principal glory of wine…
is the endless variety of its qualities and flavors."
- Hugh Johnson

In this section of the book we will quickly cover a few of the interesting beverages currently found in New England. Not everyone thought that we should include wines and other drinks made from sources other than grapes, but we wanted to convey to you everything that we found that was exciting and being created in New England. We also thought of a quote in Richard Paul Hinkle's book *Good Wine, the New Basics* that states, "wine is just grape juice." So we decided not to be wine snobs, but explorers, and tried to taste and experience everything. Here's what we found...

Fruit Wine and Spirits

There are many New England wineries that are using a variety of different fruits to create their wine. We found this to be quite understandable since New England has a great many fruit producing farms where they can use the freshest of produce. The fruit grown on each of these farms varies depending on location and the knowledge and experience of the farmers working the land. Some of the fruit currently being used to create New England wines are apples, pears, raspberries, peaches, strawberries, blueberries, cranberries, black currants, blackberries, elderberries and rhubarb. Some of these wines are also flavored with nuts, spices, honey, maple syrup or even chocolate.

Some wineries use their fruit to make a type of *Eau de Vie*. Eau de Vie is a French term that translates to "water of life." It is a spirit that has been around throughout Europe for hundreds of years. Grapes and other fruits such as pears, cherries, plums and raspberries are used to make this clear liquid. The fruit is picked at the peak of ripeness, gently crushed, yeast is added, then it is fermented, distilled and bottled very quickly to preserve the fruit flavor, and finally a clear un-oaked grape (or fruit) spirit is produced. A high quality Eau de Vie can use up to 30 pounds of fresh, ripe fruit. In ancient times, the substance was added to water for purification and also used more as medicine than a social drink. All around the world, different countries have their own varieties of Eau de Vie. In Scotland, it's whiskey, in France, it's Cognac, and in Greece, it's Ouzo. Eau de Vie is usually served chilled as an after-dinner drink.

Some of the wineries are also distilleries, using their fruit to make liqueurs. Some of the spirits being created are gin, vodka and flavored liqueurs such as Flag Hill Winery's Sugar Maple Liqueur. Some wineries are creating other useful products such as maple syrup and vanilla extract.

Below is a list of some of the New England wineries that are producing fruit wines: Jones Winery; White Silo Farm & Winery; Bartlett Maine Estate Winery; Shalom Orchard Organic Winery; Sweetgrass Farm Winery & Distillery; Winterport Winery; Nashoba Valley Winery; Obadiah McIntyre Farm Winery; Plymouth Bay Winery; Plymouth Colony Winery; Russell Orchards Farm & Winery; Diamond Hill Vineyards; Boyden Valley Winery; Charlotte Village Winery; Grand View Winery; North River Winery; Ottauquechee Valley Winery.

Below is a list of some of the New England wineries that are producing spirits: Sweetgrass Farm Winery & Distillery; Nashoba Valley Winery; Flag Hill Winery & Distillery; Nantucket Vineyard; Flag Hill Farm.

Apple Wines and Ciders

Apples are not native to America but were brought here from Canada in the early 17th century. According to history, the first apple orchard planted in New England was on Beacon Hill in Boston. After beer, apple cider is known to be the most common drink in Colonial America. Sweet cider was made from pressing the juice out of the apples and letting it age for a short time. The aging is what turns the juice to cider. When the cider is allowed to ferment, it becomes what is called "hard" cider.

Cider became very popular because apple orchards were abundant and cheap and were easier to grow than the grains needed to make beer. The cider that the early settlers drank was much different than the ciders we drink today. Theirs were very dry and did not contain much alcohol. They started adding sugar to improve the flavor and to increase the alcohol content, making cider an important export product from New England during the 18th century.

Today wineries and farms are making cider and wines from many different apple varieties. Some are going back in time to recreate those old cider flavors while others are making newer versions. The wineries are blending their apple wines with other farm flavors to bring some exciting mixes to the market. The possibilities are endless, give them a try!

Foxwhelp, Ashmead's Kernel, Bramtot Apples, Farnum Hill Ciders (Farnum Hill photos)

Below is a list of some of the New England wineries that are producing apple wines: LaBelle Winery; Bishop's Orchards Winery; Chester Hill; Russell Orchards Farm & Winery; Shalom Orchard Organic Winery; Sweetgrass Farm Winery & Distillery; Furnace Brook Winery; Grand View Winery; Ottauquechee Valley Winery; North River Winery; Diamond Hill Vineyards; Newport Vineyards; Obadiah McIntyre Farm Winery; Plymouth Winery; Russell Orchards Farm & Winery; Boyden Valley Winery.

Below is a list of some of the New England wineries that are producing ciders: Farnum Hill Ciders; Flag Hill Farm; West County Cider; Obadiah McIntyre Farm Winery; Russell Orchards Farm & Winery; Furnace Brook Winery.

Blueberry Wine

Blueberries are one of the three fruits native to New England. The other two are cranberries and Concord grapes. Some of these blueberries are being used to make wine. Most of these wines are aged in oak barrels, like grape wines, creating some very sophisticated tasting wine. Styles range from crisp and clean, to rich and zesty, and there are even some sweet dessert wines being produced.

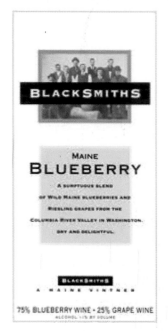

Blueberries have many health benefits. They are a good source of antioxidants, which may reduce the risk of cancer and cardio-vascular disease. They are high in vitamin C, low in calories (80 calories per cup), have almost no fat, and are a good source of manganese for bones and fiber for digestion. Recently we read (in a medical magazine while waiting at a doctor's office) that a small amount of alcohol actually improves that body's ability to absorb some of these natural benefits. Now, though we don't know if all of this is true, it made us enjoy that second glass all the more!

Below is a list of some of the New England wineries that are producing blueberry wines: Bartlett Maine Estate Winery; Chester Hill Winery; DiGrazia Vineyards; Hopkins Vineyard; Blacksmiths Winery; Cellardoor Vineyard; Shalom Orchard Organic Winery; Sweetgrass Farm Winery & Distillery; Tanguay & Son Winery; Winterport Winery; Alfalfa Farm Winery; Nashoba Valley Winery; Plymouth Colony Winery; Plymouth Winery; Russell Orchards Farm & Winery; Flag Hill Winery and Distillery; Zorvino Vineyards; Diamond Hill Vineyards; Boyden Valley Winery; Charlotte Village Winery; Grand View Winery; Ottauquechee Valley Winery.

Blueberries, Jones Winery (Jones Winery photo)

Cranberry Wine

Cranberries were first planted in New England around 1810 by Captain Henry Hall of Dennis, Massachusetts and others quickly followed his lead. Cranberry vines, once planted, can survive indefinitely. There are several vines on Cape Cod that are more than 150 years old. They do however require a few important elements to survive. These elements include acid peat soil, fresh water, sand, and a slightly long growing season that starts in April and ends in November.

Most people believe that cranberries grow in water, but this is not true. What most cranberry growers do is flood their bogs with water, which causes the berries to rise to the top, making it easier for their harvesting machines to gather the crop. Currently, cranberries are the number one food crop in Massachusetts.

Below is a list of some of the New England wineries that are producing cranberry wines: Plymouth Colony Winery; Plymouth Bay Winery; Plymouth Winery, Flag Hill Winery and Distillery; Diamond Hill Vineyards; Boyden Valley Winery; North River Winery; Zorvino Vineyards.

Plymouth Colony Winery Cranberry bog (Chris Obert photo)

Mead (Honey Wine)

Mead, made from honey, is actually one of the oldest drinks known to mankind, tracing its roots back to the mythology of the Greeks, the Vikings and the Celts. There is also evidence that some form of mead was popular during the Stone Age. But as the population grew, the number of wild bee hives decreased and the cost of honey increased. Since grapes were cheaper to grow, many civilizations switched to grape wines and mead was only available to royalty.

To make mead, honey, water and yeast are allowed to ferment for about nine months. Other fruit flavors are sometimes added, such as apples, blueberries, peaches, pears, plums and cranberries. In addition, spices such as lavender, nutmeg, vanilla and clove can be added. Mead is made in many styles such as dry, semi-dry, semi-sweet and sweet. Currently, mead is very popular with beer drinkers and people who are interested in Medieval and Renaissance history, including wedding parties with these themes.

Below is a list of some of the New England wineries that are producing meads: Piscassic Pond Winery; Plymouth Colony Winery; Bartlett Maine Estate Winery; Shalom Orchard Organic Winery; Nashoba Valley Winery.

New England, Rediscovering Its Beverage Heritage
Beer, Cider, Mead and Wine

Since the earliest explorers and colonists settled in the land now called New England, the need for thirst-quenching beverages had been foremost on their minds. The colonists, for the most part, did not drink water. After generations of bias against the polluted and contaminated waters of Europe, the settlers did not trust the rivers and streams of New England. It became common practice to brew, ferment, and heat beverages to make them safe for consumption. And consumption of beverages was what they did in abundance! Young and old, male and female, they all needed large quantities of liquids each day. They were not trying to get drunk but just trying to survive! Remember that the settlers worked on average, twelve to sixteen hours each day. These long hours made them work up quite a sweat. Their diet also contributed to their thirst. Their main sources of food were grains and cereals that were high in starch, with an occasional piece of meat or fish. The meat and fish were more often than not dried, smoked or salted, creating more thirst.

The colonists, of course, brought barrels of beverages with them but they did not last long and supply ships were not always reliable. They needed to find New England replacements for their drinking needs. The colonists would search the countryside for any native varieties of plants, fruits, vegetables and grains with which they could make their beverages. If they could not find what they were looking for they would try to plant the needed crops, such as apples or pears. The one constant problem was the lack of sugar. Wine could be easily made from grapes because of their high sugar content but other beverage sources were also needed. Importing sugar, mostly from the West Indies, was expensive and was frowned upon because of its ties to the slave trade. The colonists found their sugar in the form of honey and maple sap. Using all of these ingredients the colonists could create a wide range of fermented beverages including beer, cider, mead and wine to fulfill their needs. The assortment of flavors was incredible, as each family had their own recipes and their own methods.

Today, some of these old historic flavors are making a comeback. Wineries, micro-breweries and cider mills throughout New England are rediscovering these classic old flavors. With the abundance of fruit orchards throughout New England, flavors like rhubarb, raspberry, currant and mulled spices are already available in New England wines. Fine collections of ciders, perries and meads are also available throughout New England. And as for beers, ales, stouts and porters, there are hundreds of micro-breweries scattered across New England. The time is right to visit New England's beverage heaven and rediscover our colonial flavors.

Our Road Trips

June 18 – 20, 2007
Day 1 - Running Brook Vineyards & Winery, Inc.;
Westport Rivers Vineyard & Winery; Sakonnet Vineyards
Day 2 - Greenvale Vineyards; Newport Vineyards
Day 3 - Plymouth Bay Winery; Plymouth Winery; Plymouth Colony Winery

Running Brook Vineyards & Winery, Inc. (MA)

The first of the wineries on our trip, and the first winery to hear our idea of a New England wine book, was Running Brook Vineyards & Winery. When we pulled into the parking lot we could tell that the place was undergoing construction. We went inside and found that the tasting area was currently inside the winery work area and warehouse. We met and spoke with owner "Manny" Morais. He told us that a new tasting room was under construction and that the winery was expanding. He planned to expand his tasting area to include a large outdoor patio area and a larger warehouse.

We were told that "Premium wines from locally grown grapes" is their motto. Mr. Morais was very knowledgeable and after talking with him at length, we found that he was very much in favor of our book. Manny feels that "Southern New England has the greatest potential to make the best wines in the world." Powerful words! He had a display of his wines and offered us a tasting. We tasted them and found that he knew what he was talking about since the wines were excellent. We enjoyed his 2005 Frost Wine, 2004 Chardonnay, 2002 White Merlot, 2002 Cabernet Franc and "Celebration," their sparkling wine. After the tastings Manny was delightful and let us drive out back into the vineyards where we took a few pictures. It was the first time we were ever in a vineyard and it was very exciting.

Running Brook is known for its Chardonnay, White Merlot, its red wines, its sparkling white and dessert wine which Chris liked a lot. Manny likes to experiment with the various grapes that he grows locally. He has "high hopes for their Dartmouth winery," according to a newspaper article proudly displayed. Well, we can vouch for him, the wine was first-rate and this was only our first stop!
We bought 4 bottles: White Merlot; Celebration (Sparkling Wine); Chardonnay; 2005 Frost Wine

Running Brook Vineyards (Chris Obert photos)

Greenvale Vineyards (RI)

Greenvale Vineyards has a distinctive green "G" logo on their signs letting visitors know they have arrived at the right place. The view from the entrance and parking area is handsome and photographic. We followed the winding pathway past some oak barrels to the tasting room, which is located in an old converted barn, quite an attractive and excellent choice for a tasting and storage area. It must be quite a sight at sunset with all of the lights glowing inside! The farm is also listed on both the Rhode Island and the National Register of Historic Places, something we found very interesting. Greenvale also hosts Jazz concerts in the barn (contact winery for details,) which could be a lot of fun and something to keep in mind for a return visit.

Our hostess Shannon was wonderful, explaining to us the various 100% Estate grown wines. We tried all of the varieties, from delicate whites to spicy reds. We both agreed that our two favorites were the 2006 Vidal Blanc, which had a nice sweet smell, and Skipping Stone White, which is their signature wine.

After enjoying our wine tasting, we decided to have a picnic lunch on one of the tables provided for guests out on the grounds. Here, we relaxed, ate our lunch and took a lot of pictures to remember our visit. Even without the photos, we were never going to forget this trip. The wines have been grand and the winery's staff exceptional. We decided that a wine book on New England had to be written and there was no turning back.

We bought 3 bottles: Skipping Stone White; Vidal Blanc; Meritage

Greenvale Vineyards (Greenvale Vineyards photo)

View of the Sakonnet River from Greenvale Vineyards (Chris Obert photo)

Plym

This
this
cranl
actua
To r
swin
cranl
desci
betw

We t
bluel
Conc

Whil
occu
the c
cranl
Mass
Linc
we a
We t

Newport Vineyards (RI)

The tasting room for Newport Vineyards is in their store, which is located in a plaza. There was no mistaking it as we walked by two large wooden containers that looked like they were used for the storing or making of wine. Also parked nearby is a very distinctive purple and white Newport Vineyards mini-bus sitting in the parking lot just waiting to take the adventurous to exciting destinations!

Here, we each tasted five wines in a wide variety of styles. Nancy really enjoyed the Pinot Grigio, which had a nice aroma of apples, the Gemini (Red), which was similar to Chianti, and the Ruby Newport, a rich and classical port. Chris favored the Great White, their signature wine, the White Cap Port and the Vidal Ice Wine, both sweeter dessert wines which are his favorites. It was also here, with our hostess Carol's help, that Chris found out that he really doesn't like oak! After tasting the same Chardonnay, one fermented in oak and one in stainless steel tanks, he realized what he didn't like, and Nancy had to agree, no oak (or very little) for us! In addition to the bottles we purchased, our hotel, the Carriage House Inn, had given us a coupon for a complimentary bottle of wine, Bellevue Blush, which we brought home as well. Newport Vineyards is known as a "full service" winery with spacious grounds for hosting special occasions like rehearsal dinners and small weddings, since the vineyard is so picturesque. Their wines are also carried in a number of local liquor stores and are on the menu of some local restaurants.

We bought 4 bottles: Pinot Grigio; White Cap; Gemini; Rhody Coyote (Hard Apple Cider)

Newport Vineyards (Chris Obert photos)

Alfalfa Farm Winery (MA)

The first thing you notice when visiting Alfalfa Farm are the two large and very distinctive silos that are on the property. They are definitely a local landmark for anyone who has driven by the winery on I-95. In addition to wine tastings, Alfalfa Farm offers wine tasting parties and is a unique setting for private parties, either on the patio or under a tent (contact the winery for more details on either of these options.) They also offer harvest parties where you can help them cut the grapes right off the vines!

Prior to our visit here, we were put in touch with Hannah Adelman Menzer, with whom Chris had many conversations and who told him a lot about the winery. This was actually our second visit here. The first visit was during a "Sails & Trails" weekend, a local annual event held in September that encourages visits to all kinds of sites throughout the Merrimack Valley area, from museums and historic sites, to whale watching and guided hikes (see their website for more details www.essexheritage.org.) This was before we had the idea for a New England wine book, but we enjoyed that first visit immensely and looked forward to returning. Our host today was Richard Adelman, who is also the owner of the winery. This time we brought our daughter Shari, who was looking forward to tasting the blueberry wine, which is their signature wine. The wines were all very good.

We bought 3 bottles: Cranberry; Blueberry; Marechal Foch 2005 and were even given a recipe for Sangria using their wines:

Alfalfa Farm Sangria:
1 bottle of Marechal Foch
½ gallon orange juice
1 liter seltzer
Slices of lemons, limes and oranges

Alfalfa Farm Winery (Alfalfa Farm photo)

Red Oak Winery (MA)

The winery is a combination of a gift shop and a tasting area, with the barrel room visible through large glass windows at the rear of the store. Our hosts were Phil Clayton and Ann Milmore, who were both

pleasant and gracious during our visit. Phil first gave us a tour of the impressive barrel room, which, interestingly, also serves as a function room. While we were there, two ladies were setting up for a party they were having later that evening and were excitedly spreading out tablecloths and putting flowers on the tables. The wine barrels are all stacked and labeled with the appropriate information, including details of the oak used, the month it was aged and toasting levels used. This makes for a very unique location for a special celebration.

Red Oak buys 100% of their grapes from California and their wine making process is a combination of Bourdeaux and California styles. They make a variety of white and red dry wines, both of which have won awards in various competitions. We also brought home a jar of their Barbera Pasta Sauce, which we used when we made meatballs for our guests at our tasting held on August 18, 2007. Everyone raved about it!

We bought 2 bottles: Red Wine Reserve 2004; Barbera 2005

The Red Oak Winery tasting room/store (Red Oak photo)

Jones Winery (CT)

This winery was originally a working farm that was started in 1848. Visitors can still pick strawberries and blueberries in the summer, pumpkins in the fall and cut a Christmas tree for the holidays. The vineyard was planted in 1999, the first harvest was in 2003, and the first wine was bottled in 2004. We approached the winery by walking along a path that led past a few farm buildings and a barn, which had a very New England feel. The buildings were even painted a classic New England red color. There were lots of people in the tasting room, where there was a festive atmosphere. This was definitely one of the friendliest and most laid-back tasting experiences we had encountered. The bar was full, but everyone was sharing their opinions and chatting amiably. In fact, while we were in the middle of our tasting, more people came in and had to wait until the next "round," as the bar was already full. But seeing how much fun we were having, they didn't seem to mind the wait. The top selling wine at Jones Winery is their Woodlands White, made with Cayuga grapes. It is a lightly sweet Riesling-like wine that is very good. Everyone seemed to enjoy the Raspberry Rhapsody, which tastes like fresh berries and would be wonderful for dessert. We also tried Black Currant Bouquet with a piece of dark chocolate for a very different taste sensation. At the end of our visit, we met Christiana Jones, one of the owners, and her baby. She was very gracious and told us to contact her if we needed any more information from her or her husband, Jaime, who is the wine maker.

Paul and Delcie Thibault and Trish and Frank Genghini
at the Jones Winery (Chris Obert photo)

While we were discussing our wine book, our eyes met with another group of wine explorers. They overheard us talking about writing a book about New England wines. We told them that we were and asked them if they would like to be included in the book. They quickly posed for a picture. Their names were Paul and Delcie Thibault and Trish and Frank Genghini. Delicie and Trish are close friends, both having grown up in the same neighborhood and attended the same high school and college. Delcie and Trish don't see as much of each other as they used to, since each are now married and living in different states, but they still try to get together as much as possible. Both families enjoy visiting wineries, so while they were enjoying a weekend together they decided to visit Jones Winery. Little did they realize that we would be lurking around with our notebook and camera. Delcie told us that they had not visited Jones Winery before and were very happy that they did. They enjoyed the wines "very, very" much and now Jones Family is one of their favorite wineries. They were not the only customers that enjoyed the Jones' wine. If we remember correctly, just about every person at the tasting stood in line to buy a bottle or two. We bought three!

We bought 3 bottles: Ripton Red; Woodlands White; Raspberry Rhapsody

McLaughlin Vineyards (CT)

A long, narrow winding road leads to this winery in the woods. We were greeted by the winery dog who was very friendly. He is even on one of their wine labels for Vista Muse, a dry white wine made from Seyval Blanc grapes. It is a very pretty label with an image of the dog lying on a stone wall, very New England! We tried this variety along with Coyote Blue, a semi-dry white wine made with Aurora grapes and Snow Goose, a semi-sweet white wine made with a blend of estate grapes, as well  as Merlot 2004, a dry red wine. The winery had numerous displays of their wine bottles sitting on oak barrels throughout the store, which is actually a small cottage with rooms to wander through full of wine and gourmet food products, including their own Grade A Dark Amber Maple Syrup. We picked up a packet of shelled pumpkin seeds to nibble on while visiting. While we were walking around, we could hear a jazzy blues band playing outside under a tent by the front door. When we went out to investigate, we met the owner of the winery, Frank Carbone, sitting outside with some other guests enjoying the concert as well. The building is surrounded by pretty green shrubbery and it's in the shade, so if you go in the summer it will be nice and cool. You can relax and have a good time, maybe even bring a picnic like some of the guests we saw during our visit. In the background, behind the musicians, we could see a nice view of the vineyards shining brightly under the sun. It does not get much better than this. Sipping wine, listening to great music, all while looking out over the rows of grapes growing in the vineyard was very cool indeed!

We bought 1 bottle: Coyote Blue

McLaughlin Vineyards (Chris Obert photo)

DiGrazia Vineyards (CT)

This winery is located in a pretty gray building which you enter by walking under a large arbor with grapes growing over it. There is also a small patio area set up underneath which was very pretty with the sun shining through the vines. The wines we tasted were very high quality wines and we had a lot of fun tasting them. The owner of the vineyard, Dr. DiGrazia, is very involved in the production of high antioxidant wines. DiGrazia Vineyards offers some wines that we thought were very unusual, such as White Magnolia, a white port, Wild Blue, a blueberry wine with brandy added, and The Birches, a dessert wine made with Connecticut Bartlett pears, black walnut and aged brandy.

The Birches
DiGrazia Vineyards

The wines were a little bit more expensive than we were used to, but we bought three bottles anyway. There are still two bottles in our wine rack that we haven't opened yet as we are saving a few special bottles for a book release party. These special selections are The Birches and White Magnolia.

The staff also execelled at customer service. Because we were not sure we would reach our next destination since it was late in the day, we asked our host how to get to the next winery, White Silo Farm and Winery. The gentleman gave us a map, told us where to go to avoid construction, then called the next winery to let them know we were coming over and made sure that they would be open to accommodate out-of-state visitors. That was definitely going above and beyond! Unfortunately, we did not get his name, but we thank him just the same.

We bought 3 bottles: Harvest Spice; The Birches; White Magnolia

White Silo Farm and Winery (CT)

This winery was very easy to spot since there is a very big white silo next to the tasting area! The building, an old converted barn, is once again a distinctive New England red color. The tasting room is very quaint with an art galley also located inside. The winery often hosts art shows, rotating local artists' work on display. We were impressed with the pottery of Marcia Taylor of Newtown, Connecticut.

White Silo serves all fruit wines made from their own fresh fruit. They make all of their wines in two categories: dry and semi-sweet. This way guests are able to taste each wine and decide which style they prefer. Our hostess, Jo, was very proud of their Sangria, which Nancy tasted and was given the recipe for.

House Specialty Blackberry Sangria:
1 part Dry Rhubarb wine
1 part Sweet Blackberry wine
Serve over ice

We were also encouraged to look around. We saw the rooms used for fermentation, bottling and labeling, and were allowed to take some pictures as well. We appreciated the fact that they stayed open later for us and another group that came in after us. This was something they did even though at the time they didn't know we were in the process of writing a book.

We bought 1 bottle: Sweet Blackberry

Turtle Creek Winery (MA)

We had been looking forward to our visit to Turtle Creek for some time. Kip Kumler, the owner, was someone that we were excited to meet and talk with. We had been in communication with him via e-mail for a while prior to our visit. Kip is a very knowledgeable and scientific winemaker, grounded in classical

wine making, and striving to make great wines, which we think he does extremely well. This winery is not open to the public, and can be visited by appointment only. Kip and Tracy, the vineyard manager, were very accommodating and friendly and also very knowledgeable about wine production and the growing of grapes. They gave us our best, most comprehensive wine tour ever, from the labs and bottling area, to the wine cellar (which is his tasting room) to the vineyards themselves. We got a quick lesson on wine making and all of the techniques involved. It was all very interesting and informative! The barrel room was quite unique. It is an underground storage area with doors that open to the outside and the archway has "Turtle Creek" engraved on it. Tasting wine here was an adventure in itself and we highly recommend this visit if you get a chance.

Kip and Tracy were excellent hosts and offered to take us out to the vineyards, both on the home's property and off site at another location. We were able to see the various grape varieties growing and learn the difference in their looks. Tracy even let us taste some of the grapes off the vine, which was the first time we were allowed that opportunity. It was thrilling! This was one of the best wine learning experiences we've ever had. Kip does not sell wine at the winery but he did let us know of a few local places we could go to purchase it. We drove into downtown Concord to the Cheese Shop www.concordcheeseshop.com where we also picked up a sandwich for a nice lunch.
We bought 2 bottles: 2005 Cabernet Sauvignon; 2005 Chardonnay

Turtle Creek Winery (Chris Obert photo)

Langworthy Farm Winery (RI)

We started our adventure here the next day. Langworthy Farm is a very small winery and the tasting room had a summer beach cottage atmosphere to it, which is appropriate since it is very close to the ocean on scenic Route 1A. The winery is also a Bed and Breakfast. The tasting room is in their gift shop where, in addition to buying a bottle of wine, you can purchase a pretty wine gift basket with wine glasses, all wrapped up in cellophane and ribbon, perfect for a gift! We met with the owner, Joe Sharry, and tried a variety of his wines, including Shelter Harbor Chardonnay, an oak barrel fermented white wine, Misquamicut Merlot, a peppery red wine, and Charlestown Cabernet Franc, a dark ruby colored red wine. We also learned an interesting story behind the crooked labels we saw on some of the bottles of his Chardonnay. Joe told us that he had two vintages of Chardonnay and needed to distinguish between the two of them, so he placed the labels crooked on one vintage. It turned out to be a good seller since the customer's eye is drawn to those bottles. We thought it was so interesting that we took a picture of one of the bottles. The wine labels have an image of a large tree, which is still on the property. It is the largest Norway Maple in Rhode Island and is estimated to be 131 years old!
We bought 1 bottle: Rhody Riesling

Heritage Trail Vineyards (CT)

This winery is located in an interesting little building painted a classic New England red. The entrance is through a rustic-looking wooden door into a small, but quaint, tasting area. The wines were prominently displayed on wine racks and also on an antique cabinet in front of a model sailing ship, with descriptions of the wines displayed as well. There was a glass-enclosed sunroom with old bottles sitting on the windowsills and displays of old wine magazines for guests to take, which we did. It was very pretty and, since we visited in the fall, all the leaves had changed colors and you could see the forest in all of its splendor. There were numerous bird feeders placed outside the windows, where the birds took advantage of the generosity of the vineyard owners. During our visit, there were many birds entertaining us while we sipped our wines. There was also a fire going in the tasting room which gave it a nice cozy feel. Our hostess was Diane Powell, who allowed us to sample wines including Sweet Reserve (their best selling wine,) which is a blend of Seyval and Cayuga White grapes, Shetucket Red, which is made with Rubiana grapes, and Rochambeau Red, which is a complex blend of four grapes: Villard Noir, Chambourcin, Merlot and Cabernet Sauvignon.
We bought 1 bottle: Sweet Reserve

Heritage Trail Vineyards (Chris Obert photos)

Obadiah McIntyre Farm Winery (MA)

Upon arrival at this winery, we could tell that this was a working farm, with various farming equipment in view of the parking area. They offer pick-your-own fruit, in season, including strawberries, blueberries, peaches and apples. In the tasting area, there are many different fruit wines and ciders on display. Their bottles are very interesting with numerous styles of bottles in various colors. If you are a collector of wine bottles, this is the place to visit! We were on the way home from our Connecticut visit and we realized how close this winery was to Routes 395/290 and, since we had time and a little bit of money left in our budget, we decided to stop in. Our hostess was Kathy, a very friendly person. The wine list is very extensive, ranging from fruit wines to sparkling wines, so we had a hard time choosing wines to sample, but some of our choices were Cherry Wine, which smelled just like maraschino cherries, Frost Berry, which had an almost creamy texture to it,

and Chambourcin, which was light and fruity. During our tasting, we met a very nice couple who have family ties to our Bradford area. It seems that we always run into the nicest people on these visits!

We bought 3 bottles: Nate's Hard Cider; Nate's Razzy Apple; Frost Berry

Obadiah McIntyre Farm Winery (Chris Obert photos)

Our Second Wine Tasting - August 18, 2007

Boyden Valley Winery (VT) - Vermont Maple Reserve
Cellardoor Winery (ME) - Amorosa
Flag Hill Winery (NH) - North River Tawny Port
Greenvale Vineyards (RI) - Skipping Stone White
Jerram Winery (CT) - Marechal Foch
Jones Winery (CT) - Raspberry Rhapsody
Miranda Vineyard (CT) - Woodridge White
Newport Vineyards (RI) - White Cap
Plymouth Bay Winery (MA) - Cranberry Blush
Red Oak Winery (MA) - Barbera 2005
Running Brook Vineyards (MA) - Celebration
Russell Orchards (MA) - New England Cider
Sakonnet Vineyards (RI) - Rhode Island Red
Snow Farm Winery (VT) - Rose Red
Zorvino Vineyards (NH) - Moscato

This gathering was the largest of the three tastings, both in terms of guests attending and number of wines tasted. It was co-hosted by our friends Phil and Karen in Phil's backyard. We set up a large tent with a bar underneath to keep people out of the sun if they preferred. It was an all-day affair with plenty of varieties of food to be sampled as well as wines. One of the food offerings was meatballs in the Barbera tomato sauce from Red Oak Winery. Another was the Champagne jelly from Westport Rivers Vineyard & Winery that we served on crackers with cream cheese. Both went over well with our friends. We did try to follow the traditional method of wine tasting, moving from white to red to sweeter dessert, but it was very informal and some people had their favorites, so we did move the order around a bit. Overall, we think the day was very fun, informative to our guests and extremely useful for our research.

The results:
The Amorosa won for "Best Tasting" with many of the guests wishing that we had a second bottle to open. It was described by many as "the best." Celebration got high marks and people seemed to like the idea of having a sparkling wine included in the tasting. The Rhode Island Red also got very high marks, earning comments such as "excellent, especially oak," and "best red."

Everyone was eagerly awaiting the opening of the North River Tawny Port so that they could try some of the wine that was contained in this old-styled bottle, and they were not disappointed! The Tawny Port got extremely high points, with a few people asking directions to Flag Hill Winery, which was not too far up the road from where we were having this tasting. Some comments on this wine were "very rich," "nice warmth" and "best of the night."

The two wines that caused the most conversation were the New England Cider and the Vermont Maple Reserve. People had mixed opinions about the flavor of the wines made from apples. It was interesting to watch as some guests passed up the wines while others quickly took a second serving. We found it informative as it proved that everyone's taste is different.

We opened the Raspberry Rhapsody last and everyone liked it. We did not finish the bottle but served it again the following day over fresh fruit and vanilla ice cream.

Our Third Wine Tasting - September 22, 2007

Alfalfa Farm (MA) - Blueberry
Boyden Valley Winery (VT) - Blueberry Wine
DiGrazia Vineyards (CT) - Harvest Spice
Flag Hill Winery (NH) - 2006 Cayuga White
Flag Hill Winery (NH) – Heritage White
Greenvale Vineyards (RI) - Vidal Blanc
Haight-Brown Vineyard (CT) - Picnic Red
Nashoba Valley (MA) - Perry Wine
Newport Vineyards (RI) - Gemini
Plymouth Colony Winery (MA) - Cayuga
Sakonnet Vineyards (RI) - Vidal Blanc

This tasting was a little bit different from the first two. This time we wanted to try a "horizontal" type head-to-head tasting between two of the same types of wines from two different New England wineries. We chose a variety of styles, from whites to reds to dessert, in an attempt to cover all ranges. We also wanted the tasting to be a "blind" tasting, where the guests were not allowed to see the label. Each guest was given two identical glasses, one with a wine charm on the stem and one without. (During our many visits, we had accumulated a lot of wine glasses from the various wineries, so this was very easy to set up!) The guests were not shown the labels, and were only told what type of wine they would be trying. Everyone had a clipboard for their notes and the votes were tallied at the end. This was a very fun way to taste the wines, as we're sure our guests would agree. In the end, we both really enjoyed this tasting and would like to do more side by side comparisons of New England wines, as well as other wines from around the world!

The following two pages will give you a description (taken from the wineries themselves) of the wines in our blind head-to-head New England wine tasting.

We would also like to take a moment to let you know that there are books out there to help you host your own tasting parties. Two books that we found helpful with our wine tastings were Simon Woods' *I Don't Know Much About Wine... but I Know What I Like* and Michael Broadbent's *Wine Tasting*. Also, it may be helpful to have a few general wines books available for guests to peruse during the tastings. For example, Karen MacNeil's *The Wine Bible* is full of information your guests may enjoy and Danny May and Andy Sharpe's *The Everything Wine Book* is also full of interesting facts and ideas. One book that we always carried around with us was Tom Stevenson's book *101 Essential Tips – Wine*. Anytime we had a question, we could quickly look it up in this handy pocket-sized book.

Vidal Blanc (Chris Obert photo)

Sakonnet Vineyards (RI) Vidal Blanc - Our Vidal grapes were harvested in mid-October. The classic floral, fruity up-front nose of this wine fools your palate into assuming it has a sweeter style. But in actuality, the finish is very dry - reminiscent of Pinot Grigio. Our 2005 Vidal Blanc was 100% stainless steel fermented at an average temperature of 50°F for two months. Vidal Blanc is Sakonnet's signature wine.

Greenvale Vineyards (RI) Vidal Blanc - This grape is a wonderful French American hybrid that produces an extremely aromatic and pleasantly flavored wine. It is a delicious bright wine, especially good with ham, salads, cheeses, and spicy foods. Medium dry. Fermented in stainless steel.

Cayuga (Chris Obert photo)

Flag Hill Winery (NH) Cayuga White - A bright semi-sweet white, layered with citrus & exotic fruit with a well-balanced acidity that lingers nicely. Great with seafood, poultry and spicy foods.

Plymouth Colony Winery (MA) Cayuga - A semi-sweet white wine similar to a German Riesling.

Blueberry (Chris Obert photo)

Alfalfa Farm Winery (MA) Blueberry - An Alfalfa Farm classic. Made entirely from wild Maine blueberries, this wine comes in semisweet or dry versions with a smooth fruit finish. Can be enjoyed as a table wine or dessert wine.

Boyden Valley Winery (VT) Blueberry Wine - A semi-sweet port style blueberry wine made from low bush blueberries and sold in a unique cobalt blue collectors bottle.

Red Table Wine (Chris Obert photo)

Haight-Brown Vineyard (CT) Picnic Red - A medium bodied red wine, made from the Marechal Foch grape variety. To enjoy on a picnic or on most occasions.

Newport Vineyards (RI) Gemini Red - A dry medium-bodied and delightfully smooth red wine with a peppery finish and a hint of oak.

Before we list the results of the contests, we would like to note that when asked, all of our guests stated that each of the wines in the contests were good enough that they would buy a bottle even when they liked one of the two wines better than the other. For some of the tasters, they had to go back and forth a few times before they could pick a winner. Everyone congratulated us on our choices of wines for this head-to-head competition. So, congratulations to all of the wineries for producing agreeable wines!

The results:
Sakonnet Vineyards' Vidal Blanc won for "Best Vidal Blanc" in the only unanimous decision. It also won for "Best Wine of the Day," and was described as "sweeter." Greenvale Vineyard's Vidal Blanc was described by one guest as "tart, dry."

Plymouth Colony's Cayuga won for "Best Cayuga" and was described as having a "thicker texture, apple flavor and aroma." Flag Hill Winery's 2006 Cayuga White earned the comment "mild, light, drier."

Boyden Valley's Blueberry Wine won for "Best Blueberry" earning comments such as "good fruit aroma." Alfalfa Farm's Blueberry was described as "sweeter, lighter in color, fruitier."

Haight-Brown's Picnic Red won for "Best Red" and was described as "more bite, peppery, oaky." Newport Vineyard's Gemini was described by one person as "smooth, milder, sweeter."

Sakonnet Vineyards (Janet Bell photo)

When the head-to-head wine challenges were over, we also offered a few other choices for our guests to taste. The Heritage White received high marks for a white wine and the Perry Wine earned high marks as a mixer. We opened the Harvest Spice last but, unfortunately, it did not go over very well. We had forgotten our lesson from our first tasting. It was a hot day and the spices in the wine were too heavy for the day's heat. It did, however, go over quite well the following evening as we sat around a fire on a cool September night.

New England Wine Trails

New Hampshire in autumn (NDC photo)

"Once you fall in love with wine,
there is no end to the pleasure and interest it provides."
- Marvin R. Shanken

New England has three well established wine trails that we are aware of. The first is **The Coastal Wine Trail of Southern New England**. It includes four Rhode Island wineries: Newport Vineyards; Greenvale Vineyards; Langworthy Farm Winery; and Sakonnet Vineyards. It also includes three Massachusetts wineries: Westport River Vineyard & Winery; Truro Vineyards; and Running Brook Vineyards. You can pick up brochures on this wine trail at any of the local tourist stops or you can visit their website at www.CoastalWineTrail.com for more information.

If you are looking for an interesting way to experience the Coastal Wine Trail, why not try a tour? One tour, Vines to Wines, Toast the Coast, Educational Tours and Tastings, offers a full day of wine tasting along the Coastal Wine Trail with small intimate tours (with a picnic lunch) for up to six guests. Their motto is "Why drive when you can ride?" You can get more information on their tours at www.vinestowinestours.com/home.

The second wine trail is the **Rhode Island Wine Trail**. It includes the four Rhode Island wineries listed above in the Coastal Wine Trail: Newport Vineyards; Greenvale Vineyards; Langworthy Farm Winery; and Sakonnet Vineyards but adds one more Rhode Island winery: Diamond Hill Vineyards. You can visit the Rhode Island Division of Agriculture at www.RIgrown.ri.gov for more information on Rhode Island wineries.

The third established New England wine trail is **Connecticut's Wine Trail**. The trail boasts fifteen wineries and is divided into East and West trail loops. The East Loop has eight wineries: Sharpe Hill Vineyard; Heritage Trail Vineyards; Jonathan Edwards Winery;

101

Coastal Wine Trail of Southern New England

Running Brook Vineyards, 335 Old Fall River Road, North Dartmouth, MA 02747
Truro Vineyards, 11 Shore Road (Route 6A), North Truro, MA 02652
Westport Rivers Vineyard & Winery, 417 Hixbridge Road, Westport, MA 02790
Greenvale Vineyards, 582 Wapping Road, Portsmouth, RI 02871
Langworthy Farm Winery, 308 Shore Road, Route 1A, Westerly, RI 02891
Newport Vineyards, 909 East Main Road, Route 138, Middletown, RI 02842
Sakonnet Vineyards, 162 West Main Road, Little Compton, RI 02827

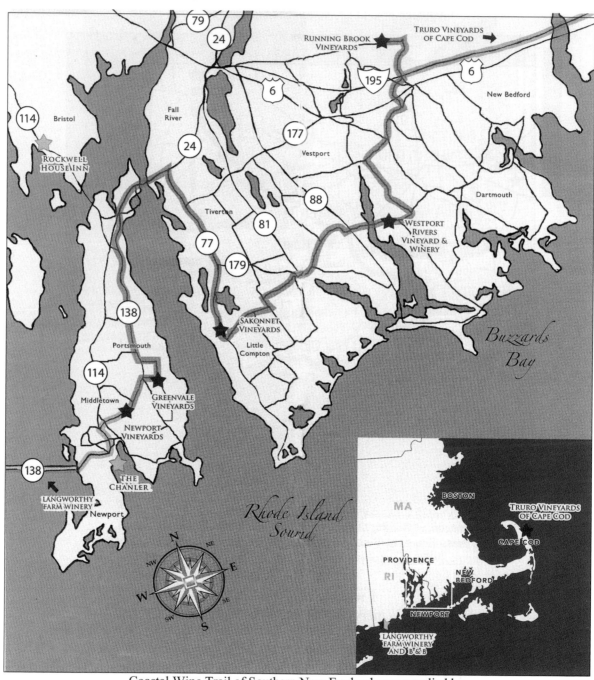

Coastal Wine Trail of Southern New England map supplied by
The Coastal Winegrowers of Southern New Engalnd www.CoastalWineTrail.com
The Commonwealth of Massachusetts www.MassVacation.com
Newport County Convention & Visitor's Bureau www.gonewport.com
Southeastern Massachusetts Convention & Visitors Bureau www.bristol-county.org

Rhode Island Wine Trail

Diamond Hill Vineyards, 3145 Diamond Hill road, Cumberland, RI 02804
Greenvale Vineyards, 582 Wapping Road, Portsmouth, RI 02871
Langworthy Farm Winery, 308 Shore Road, Route 1A, Westerly, RI 02891
Newport Vineyards, 909 East Main Road, Route 138, Middletown, RI 02842
Sakonnet Vineyards, 162 West Main Road, Little Compton, RI 02827

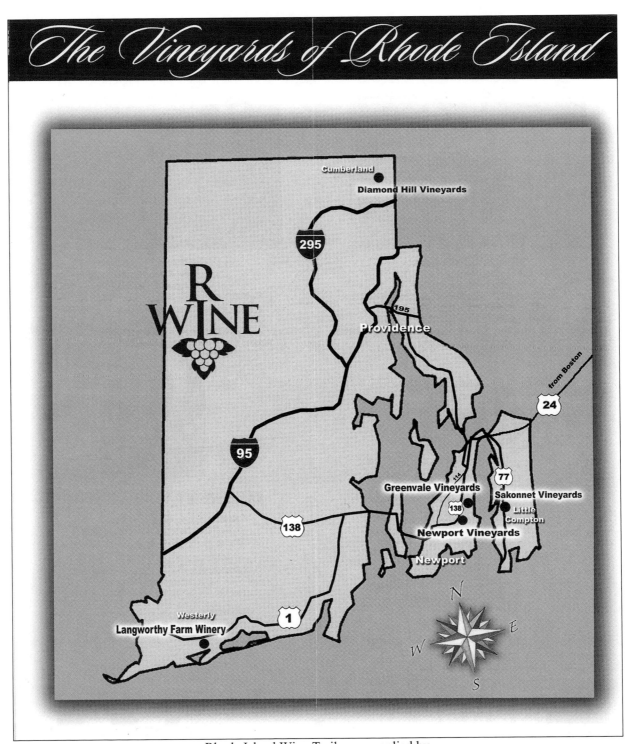

Rhode Island Wine Trail map supplied by
The Rhode Island D.E.M. Division of Agriculture www.RIgrown.ri.gov

Green Mountain Wine Trail

Farnum Hill Ciders, 98 Poverty Lane, Lebanon, NH, 03766
Flag Hill Farm, 135 Ewing Road, Vershire, VT 05079
Ottauquechee Valley Winery, 5573 Woodstock Rd. Route 4, Quechee, VT 05059

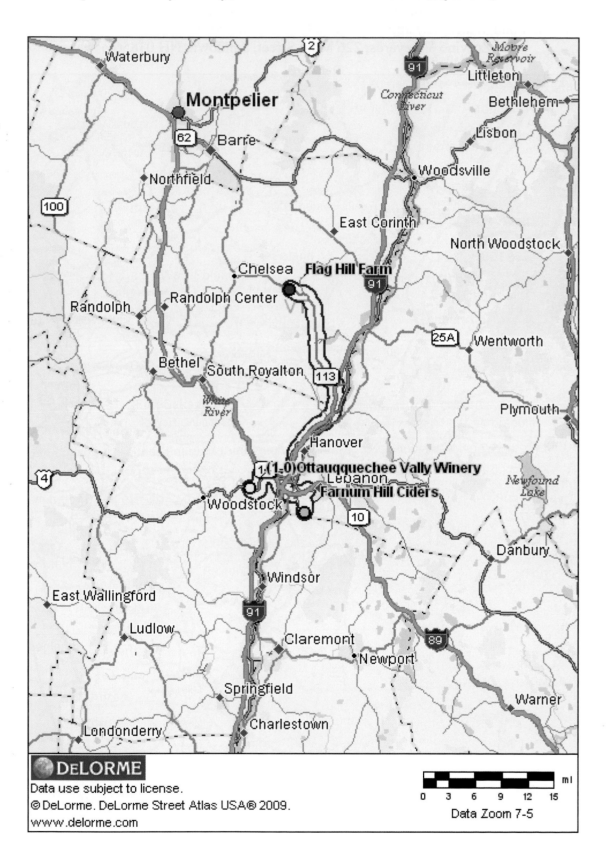

Lake Champlain Wine Trail

Boyden Valley Winery, 70 Vermont Route 104, Cambridge, VT 05444
Charlotte Village Winery, 3968 Greenbush Road, Charlotte, VT 05445
Grand View Winery, Max Gray Road, East Calais, VT 05650
Shelburne Vineyard, 310 Beach Road, Shelburne, VT 05482
Snow Farm Vineyard, 190 West Shore Road, South Hero, VT 05486

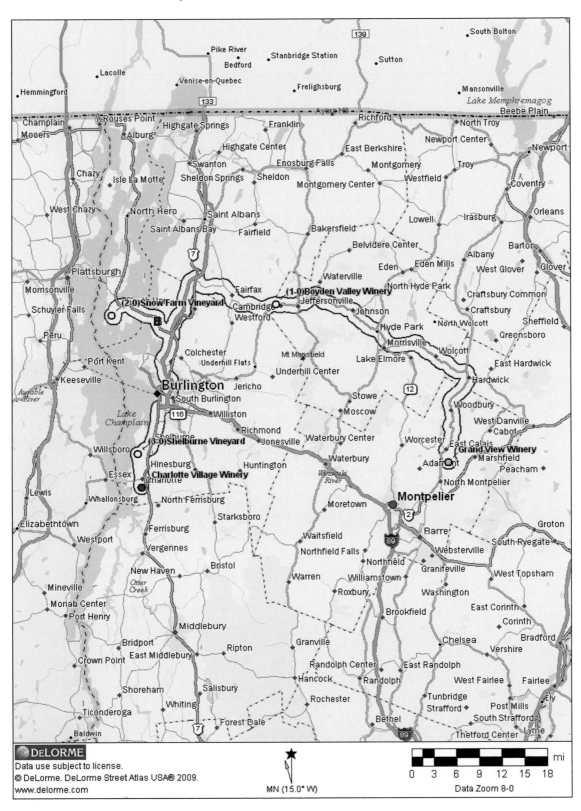

The Berkshires Wine Trail

North River Winery, 201 VT Route 112 River Road, Jacksonville, VT 05342
Chester Hill Winery, 47 Lyon Hill Road, Chester, MA 01011
Furnace Brook Winery, 508 Canaan Road, Richmond, MA 01254
Hardwick Vineyard & Winery, 3305 Greenwich Road, Hardwick, MA 01037
Les Trois Emme Winery, 8 Knight Road, New Marlborough, MA 01230
Obadiah McIntyre Farm Winery, Charlton Orchards Farm, 44 Old Worcester Road, Charlton, MA 01507
West Country Cider, 45 N Catamount Hill Road, Colrain, MA 01340

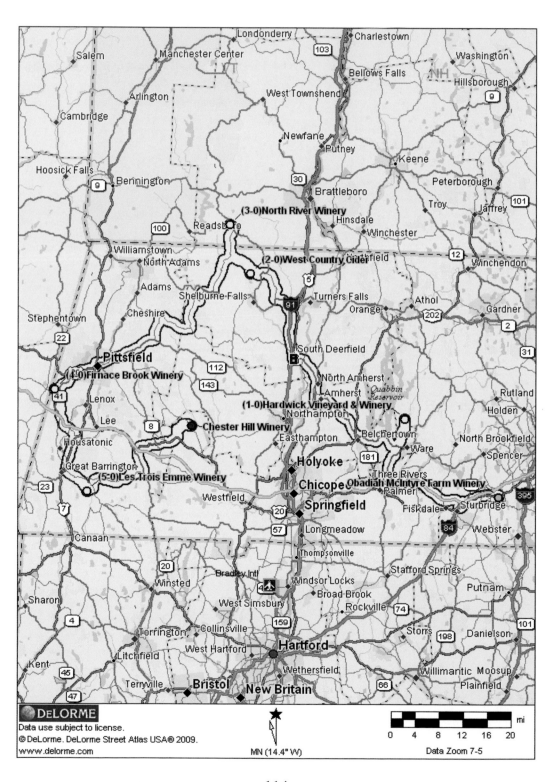

Greater Boston Wine Trail

Alfalfa Farm Winery, 267 Rowley Bridge Road, Topsfield, MA 01983
Broad Hill Vineyards, 583 Winter Street, Holliston, MA 01746
Cantina Bostonia, 30 Germania Street, Ste A, Jamaica Plain, MA 02130
Nashoba Valley Winery, 100 Wattaquadoc Hill Road, Bolton, MA 01740
Neponset Winery, 50 Kearney Road, Needham, MA 02494
Red Oak Winery, 325 North Main Street, Middleton, MA 01949
Russell Orchards Farm & Winery, 143 Argilla Road, Ipswich, MA 01938
Turtle Creek Winery (by appointment only), 28 Beaver Pond Rd, Lincoln, MA 01773

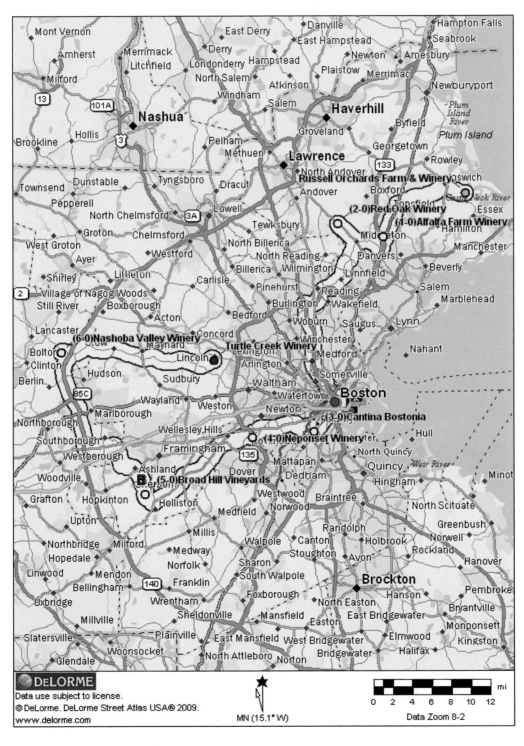

Cape Cod and the Islands Wine Trail

Cape Cod Cellars, 55 Linden Tree Lane, Chatham, MA 02633
Cape Cod Winery, 681 Sandwich Road, East Falmouth, MA 02536
Chicama Vineyards, 191 Stoney Hill Roads, West Tisbury, MA 02575 (Closed Sept. 2008)
Nantucket Vineyard & Triple Eight Distillery, 5 Bartlett Farm Road, Nantucket, MA 02584
Plymouth Bay Winery, 114 Water Street, Plymouth, MA 02362
Plymouth Colony Winery, 56 Pinewood Road, Plymouth, MA 02360
Plymouth Winery, 170 Water Street, Plymouth, MA 02360
Truro Vineyards, 11 Shore Road Route 6A, North Truro, MA 02652

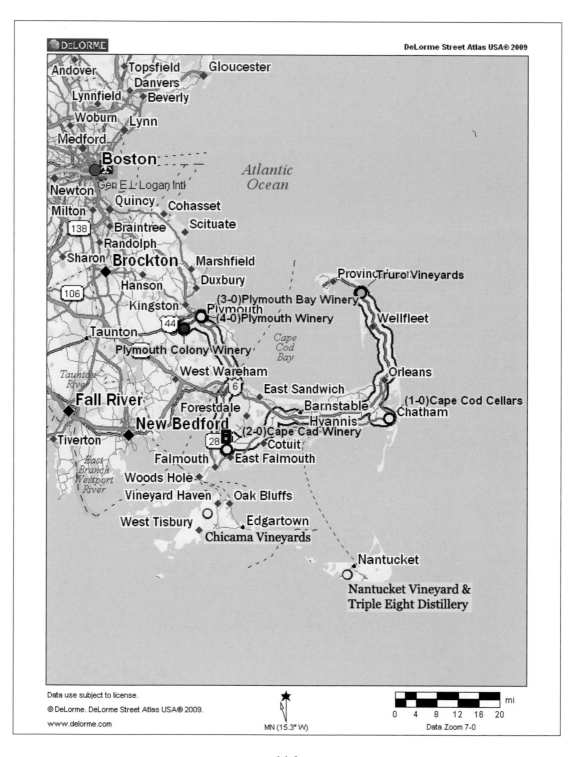

The Future of New England Vineyards & Wineries

Autumn in New England (NDC photo)

"Good wine is a necessity of life for me."
- Thomas Jefferson

Well, here we are at the end of Part One of the book. We hope that you have found the book to be fun and informative so far. In this section of the book we want to talk about the only two problems that we had while we were working on this book. The first problem was a good problem, change. Everything was changing as we researched this book, but changing for the better. Many New England websites were improved during the time we worked on the book. Also, many of the wineries were expanding and some were opening for the first time. This was good for you, the visitor, but hard for us to keep up with since the information kept changing. Another example of change is grapes. As we mentioned before, the wineries are planting more varieties of grapes than they have done before. Included in this book is a partial list of some of the wine grapes currently being grown in New England. This list is not complete and should not be considered as anything more than a sampling of what is currently being planted. Corot Noir, Frontenac Gris, LaCrosse and Muscat Valvin are a few of the other varieties growing in New England that were not covered. Over time, the list of grapes will change as the New England climate changes, for what works well in one microclimate may not work well elsewhere. Also, one bad winter can wipe out years of hard work! So things can change quickly.

The growing of wine grapes is a tricky proposition. The list will also change as new and better techniques are developed to grow wine grapes in the diverse environments of New England. Also remember that new and exciting grape varieties are constantly being developed to take advantage of the unique conditions of New England. Who knows what intriguing combinations of grapes could be growing in the near future?

117

New and Not Listed New England Wineries

While writing this book many changes occurred in the New England wine industry, with wineries opening and some closing. Some wineries we could not find information on or did not respond to our inquiries. One new winery, the Black Dog Vineyards, in Salisbury, New Hampshire has a web page www.theblackdogvineyard.com detailing their progress as a winery. It lists step-by-step the evolution of their vineyard and winery. It is a good example of what all new wineries must go through. We wish them luck. The following is a quick list of changes and additions to the New England winery landscape as well as wineries missing from this book.

Connecticut
Holmberg Orchards, Gales Ferry
Maugle Sierra Vineyards, Ledyard
Rosedale Vineyards, Simsbury
Savino Vineyards, Woodbridge
Sunset Meadow Vineyard, Goshen

Maine
Prospect Hill Winery, Lebanon
Royal River Winery, Yarmouth
The Sows Ear Winery, Brookeville

Massachusetts
Alfina Winery, Ashburnham
Chicama Vineyards, West Tisbury (closed)
Willow Spring Vineyards, Haverhill

New Hampshire
Barnett Hill Vineyard, Walpole

New Hampshire (cont.)
The Black Dog Vineyards, Salisbury
Garp Family Winery, Loudon
Poocham Hill Winery, West Moreland
Silver Mountain Ciders, Lempster
Stone Gate Vineyard, Gilford
Vintner's Cellar of Bedford, Bedford
Vintner's Cellar, Portsmouth

Rhode Island
Block Island Vineyards, Block Island (closed?)
Shelalara Vineyards & Winery, Coventry (closed?)

Vermont
Apple Tree Farm Wines, Chester
Joseph Cerniglia Winery, Proctorsville
L'Abeille Honey Winery, Stowe
Putney Mountain Winery, Putney

Other New England wine-related companies of interest:

New England Wine Cellars LLC in West Cornwall, CT
This company provides artistic design and expert installation of commercial and residential wine cellars and display systems.
www.NewCellars.com

The Oxford Wine Room – On Line
A web page that claims to be "The information source for wine and fine dining in New England." www.OxfordWineRoom.com

Passport Wine Club (Geerlings & Wade) in Canton, MA
This is a membership wine club where you receive newsletters and wine guides, along with bottles of wine from around the world, every month.
www.GeerWade.com

We Teach Wine in Providence, RI
This is a business that teaches wine to the public through classes and also creates wine events for corporations. www.WeTeachWine.com

More Information on New England and Its Wines

For additional and up-to-date information we recommend the following publications and webpages:

New England Wine Gazette (newspaper)
c/o The Recorder Publishing Co.
17 – 19 Morristown Rd.
Bernardsville, NJ 07924
Business Office (908) 766-3900 Ext. 52

The New England "Edible" magazines:
Edible Boston, Edible Cape Cod, Edible Green Mountains (Vermont), *Edible Nutmeg* (Connecticut), *Edible Rhody* (Rhode Island), *Edible White Mountains* (New Hampshire)
Edible Communities
369 Montezuma Avenue, Ste. 577
Santa Fe, NM 87501

University of Massachusetts Amherst's New England Wine Grape Growers Resource Center www.NewEnglandWineGrapes.org. Their website "has been created to provide these vineyard wineries access to resources to assist in the production of high quality grapes and wines (and) to help residents and visitors to New England learn more about this vibrant part of our agricultural community. Visit some of our New England Vineyard Wineries and enjoy a unique taste of New England."

The New Hampshire Winery Association is a newly formed organization devoted to the New Hampshire Wine Industry www.NHWineryAssociation.com.

Yankee (magazine) founder Robb Sagendorph was "so inspired by the spirit of New England that he started a magazine about it. Independence, integrity, ingenuity, perseverance, self-sufficiency, community - these are the values that have made both New England and Yankee Publishing successful."
1121 Main Street, Dublin, NH 03444, (603) 563-8111 www.YankeeMagazine.com

Wine bottles, Sakonnet Vineyards (Janet Bell photo)

121

Part Two

Connecticut

Chamard Vineyards

Chamard Vineyards
115 Cow Hill Road
Clinton, CT 06413
(860) 664-0299
www.Chamard.com

Chamard Vineyards is dedicated to producing fine wines from classic European wine grapes. A blend of time-honored wine making techniques and state of the art winery equipment are used to create world class wines. The main focus at Chamard is on Chardonnay, the most noble white wine grape variety in the world and the best variety that grows in the region.

The vineyards spread across 40 acres of gently sloping fields along the southern Connecticut coast, just two miles from Long Island Sound. The 20 acres of established vines include the varieties Chardonnay, Cabernet Sauvignon, Pinot Noir, Merlot and Cabernet Franc. Chamard's classic New England styled winery features finely crafted stonework using field stones from the property and wooden beams milled from trees harvested from the property. Chamard benefits from a unique micro-climate influenced greatly by Long Island Sound. Located two miles from the sound and six miles from the mouth of the Connecticut River, this maritime climate produces mild winter temperatures and a long, warm growing season. The rich, stony soil, gently sloping land and moderate climate provide an ideal environment for the growing of European wine grapes.

Combining his love of nature, his interest in genetics, and his passion to predict, Dr. Rothberg purchased the leading vineyard in Connecticut to push the frontiers of winemaking. Originally Incorporated in 1983 by the Chairman and CEO of Tiffany and CO., Dr. Rothberg found in Chamard vineyards a foundation of grace and elegance that would form the basis for even finer wines.

The first vines were planted in the spring of 1984, a 5.5 acre vineyard consisting primarily of Chardonnay with a small quantity of Cabernet Sauvignon and Pinot Noir. From 1986 through 1992 the remaining acreage was prepared and planted, for a combined total of 20 acres. In the summer of 1988, the winery was constructed and Chamard became a licensed farm winery. The first wine, a 1988 Chardonnay was released for sale in November of 1989. Current production is 6,000 cases annually.

An old-world adage, but also the feeling of our General Manager and Winemaker, Larry McCulloch, who painstakingly cares for the 20 acres of vines. During the winter months each vine is carefully hand-pruned to maintain the proper crop levels and ensure plant vigor. In the spring the growing vines are trained onto a special trellis system where the emerging buds, and later the clusters, are carefully thinned to an optimum level. Throughout the summer the vines are positioned along the trellis wires and periodically hedged to enhance growth and improve fruit quality. Through active vine management and carefully controlled fruit production, we are able to maximize the varietal character in our wines.

The elegant tasting room features a large fieldstone fireplace, natural wood surfaces and antiques. The deck offers a panoramic view of the vineyard with its rolling acres of lush vines; hand built stone walls lining the fields and a beautiful pond with a cascading fountain. The winery was completed in 1988. Its classic New England design features finely crafted stonework using fieldstones from the property. The staff is both friendly and knowledgeable.

Taste and purchase our handcrafted award-winning wines, including our spectacular Estate Reserve Wines and older vintages. Take advantage of case discounts and become a member of our Vintage Patron's Club for discounts all year and invitations to private VIP releases and barrel tastings. The Chamard Vineyard Tour takes you through the winery for an informative look at our wine making process. Enjoy a tasting of five Chamard wines in the tasting room overlooking the vineyards. Bring lunch to pair with wine by the glass on the deck or bring a blanket and picnic by the pond. Enjoy the regions best locally grown and produced food at the Farmer's Market hosted by Chamard with live music from 12:00 to 3:00 pm. The setting is ideal for private events, a French country get away on the Connecticut shoreline. Tasting the wines makes it clear why Chamard has won "Best Connecticut Wine," *Connecticut Magazine*, for ten consecutive years.

2003 Estate Reserve CHARDONNAY –
A rich, viscous Chardonnay bursting with unctuous flavors, hints of ripe melon, pineapple and other tropical fruits. Bound to attract a lot of fans. With low acidity and very pronounced aromatics, this is a luscious Burgundian style Chardonnay.

STONE COLD WHITE –
"This new unoaked, non-malolatic or 'naked' chardonnay pushes the limits of east coast chardonnay to new heights of expression. A rich, vibrant blast of citrus and lemon flavors are framed by a seductive bracing acidity creating a new wine which will change the way the world thinks of Connecticut wine." Henry Ponzio, Wine Consultant.

2005 CABERNET SAUVIGNON –
Deep color, with aromas of summer roses, raspberry, cherry and a touch of oak. Rich, powerful flavors, with a lean style typical of European vinifera grown in the North East. A blend of five varietals including, 78% Cabernet Sauvignon, 10% Merlot, 7% Cabernet Franc, 4% Petite Verdot and 2% Pinot Noir.

2005 MERLOT –
The dark, rich, almost black raspberry color hints as to what is to come in this right bank Bordeaux style red. This wine is predominately merlot based, bolstered by some cabernet sauvignon and spiced with cabernet franc. The aromas are of earth and coffee grinds followed by flavors of bittersweet chocolate covered raspberry all held together with firm tannins and pleasing food friendly acidity.

2004 Estate Reserve Cabernet Franc –
Ripe fruit aromas and spicy, red berry flavors complimented by a touch of toasty oak. Medium-bodied and well-balanced with good tannins and a spicy finish. Blended with 15% Merlot and 10% Cabernet Sauvignon.

2006 PINOT BLANC –
A Pinot Blanc with floral aromas of citrus and lime, followed by flavors of apple and melon. Vibrant with hints of minerals and a refreshing crisp finish.

Connecticut Valley Winery

Connecticut Valley Winery
1480 Litchfield Turnpike (Route 202)
New Hartford, CT 06057
(860) 489-9463
www.CTValleyWinery.com

Connecticut Valley Winery, located in Connecticut's picturesque Litchfield County, is owned and operated by Anthony and Judith Ferraro. With a passion for offering the highest quality wines, while preserving all the charm of a small, family owned winery, the Ferraros offer an unmatched wine experience in one of the most beautiful and intimate of New England locales.

A passion for perfection: Using local hybrid grapes and hybrid grape blends, Anthony combines his extensive knowledge of fine wine and wine-making techniques to produce distinctive blends that are truly unique to the region.

Stop by and see us: Visit our vineyards, sample our distinctive wines, browse our unique gifts, and experience the warm and welcoming environment that defines Connecticut Valley Winery. You're welcome to bring a light lunch or snack and relax on the deck or by the fireplace with your wine purchase. You just might find Anthony in the vineyards making sure his grapes ripen to perfection.

Consider having your party at Connecticut Valley Winery. Call for information.

A commitment to fine wine:
This year's harvest brings to the table a variety of limited-edition wines that will delight the most distinctive palates:

REDS:
Chianti – A blend of six varieties of grapes fermented and aged to produce this semi-dry table wine. Connecticut Valley Winery is the only winery in the region to make Chianti.

Ruby Lite – A blend of red and white hybrid grapes gives this wine its rich ruby color. The perfect compliment to meat, fish or pasta dishes.

Watch for our new Cabernet debuting late spring 2008!

ESTATE Bottled:
Midnight – Deep, dark and mysterious, a tangy table wine made from Frontenac hybrid grapes.

Deep Purple – Royal, proud and sophisticated, a mellow table wine produced from Chamborcin, a French hybrid grape.

Dolce Vita – A white grape wine, lightly fermented to create this sweet, low alcohol, low acidity table wine. Serve chilled.

WHITES:
Chardonel – A white hybrid grape with the characteristics of Chardonnay and Seyval produces this smooth, refreshing white wine.

White Sparkling Wine – A blend of Chardonel and Cayuga grapes, fermented and aged to produce a pleasant, light, sparkling wine. Serve chilled.

Spumonte Muscato – A light, white sparkling wine, fruity and smooth, produced from Muscato grapes. Serve chilled.

Dolce Vita – A white grape wine, fermented to create this sweet, low alcohol, low acidity table wine. Serve chilled.

FRUIT:
Just Peachy – A delightful white grape wine infused with the essence of peaches. Serve chilled.

Raspberry Delight – A white grape wine infused with the essence of red raspberries. Serve chilled.

131

DiGrazia Vineyards

DiGrazia Vineyards
131 Tower Rd.
Brookfield, CT 06804
(203) 775-1616
www.Digrazia.com

DiGrazia Vineyards was founded in 1978 and is dedicated to producing premium wines of quality and unique variety. Over 15 wines are offered, ranging from dry to sweet, using estate grown grapes, local fruit and honey. Our two vineyard sites are established on high sloping hills to maximize growing potential and grapes grown lead to crisp, flavorful wines. Nine varieties of premium hybrid and native American wine grapes are planted.

Dr. Digrazia, founder and winemaker, is widely known for his clean, crisp style of winemaking and his innovative flair. He has been intensively involved in the production of high antioxidant wines. A wide range of table and dessert wines are offered at DiGrazia Vineyards including whites, blushes, reds, nouveau, spiced pumpkin, red and white port, and other unique wines. They are also available in Conneticut Package stores and by mail.

Visitors can enjoy a guided winery tour and wine tasting, country gift shop, and picnic area on our arbor patio.

Winners Cup Dry – A mellow, full-bodied Vidal Blanc aged in white American oak. A pleasant dinner wine. 2003 American Wine Society Competition - Silver Medal.

Wind Ridge - A semi-dry Seyval Blanc. Light and crisp with a hint of sweetness. Seyval is known for it's apple-like flavors.

Honey Blush - A semi-dry honey-grape wine. Lighter styled with a honeyed, lingering aftertaste. No added sulfites.

Anastasia's Blush - A full flavored blush with heavy fruit flavors. Sweet and tangy.

William's Sonnet - A white grape wine blushed with raspberry. Just a hint of tartness on the finish. A wonderful sipping wine.

Newbury - A nouveau styled red wine full of the fresh fruit flavor of its vintage season. A perfect compliment to holiday meals. Available in November and December only.

Fieldstone Reserve - A dry, medium-bodied red table wine aged in white American oak. Cherry and black currant flavors. Serve with steak and Italian foods. 2003 American Wine Society Competition - Bronze Medal.

Autumn Spice - White grapes are fermented with sugar pumpkin and honey, then lightly spiced with cinnamon, ginger, nutmeg and cloves. Aromatic with a hint of sweetness. 2006 "Big E" New England Wine Competition - Gold Medal.

Harvest Spice - A blush styled wine fermented with sugar pumpkin, honey and spices. Mellow, sweeter and spicier flavor. Can be served warm.

Yankee Frost - A sweet Vidal Blanc. Complex with intense fruit flavor and a hint of citrus on a long finish. The grapes were harvested during a frosty October morning in the style of an ice wine. (11% alc/vol) 2004 American Wine Society Competition - Silver Medal

The Birches - A blend of CT Bartlett pears, black walnut and aged brandy. Elegant and distinctive. (18% alc/vol)

White Magnolia - A light white port. White grape and brandy with layers of fruit flavors. (15.8% alc/vol) 2006 "Big E" New Wine Competition - Silver Medal; 2003 American Wine Society Competition - Bronze Medal.

Winterberry - A blend of grape, raspberry, black currant, honey, citrus brandy. A rich and delightful dessert wine. (16% alc/vol) (375 ml bottle only) 2006 "Big E" New England Wine Competition - Gold Medal.

Blacksmith Port - A ruby styled red port. Medium bodied with superb concentration of spicy fruit flavors and soft tannins. A smooth lingering finish. A favorite! (18% alc/vol) 2005 Amenti Del Vino Wine Competition - Double Gold Medal.

Wild Blue Too - A delicious blend of blueberry and CT apple with a high antioxidant level. (12% alc/vol)

Gouveia Vineyards

Gouveia Vineyards
1339 Whirlwind Hill Rd.
Wallingford, CT 06492
(203) 265-5526
www.GouveiaVineyards.com

Gouveia Vineyards is a great little getaway for visitors who may want to sample our fine wines or simply enjoy a glass or bottle of their favorite one. Over the past several months, Gouveia Vineyards

entered some of its wines in a number of international competitions on the eastern coast and has received several awards. We are particularly proud of this, as we competed against some well-known wineries such as Mondavi, Chateau St. Michele, Gallo, and Kendall Jackson. Encouraged by these awards, Gouveia Vineyards continues to be committed to producing mature and flavorful wines.

We have good news for the fans of our Chardonnay Stainless Steel wine---IT'S BACK! So come visit, enjoy the view, have a glass or purchase some to take home. Gouveia Vineyards is also pleased to announce the completion of its newly expanded tasting room. Not only does this beautiful new room provide more seating for our visitors, but it now offers twice the view of the surrounding countryside. Rolling hills, fiery sunsets, and of course, wonderful vineyards are all a part of this view.

We wish everyone a wonderful year, and we look forward to seeing you soon. We also want to thank all our visitors for their patience and understanding during the construction of the expanded tasting room. Now that it's finished, we hope everyone enjoys it as much as we enjoy having visitors at the winery!

Thank you for your continued support!
Owners: Joe & Lucy Gouveia
WineMaker: Joe Gouveia

Come watch the sunset by the warmth of the fire while enjoying a glass of our wine. We're proud to offer our fine wines, spectacular views and hospitality to help you unwind and relax. We invite you to bring a lunch basket with you while you sample our wines. We offer our wines by the bottle or by the glass and also offer a wine tasting to help you choose the wine that is most to your taste. Visitors are not allowed to bring any other beverages onto to the premises. Bottled water and soda are also available for sale.

Whirlwind Rosé –
A semi-sweet, crisp blend of both vinifera and hybrid grapes, emoting hints of mulled apple spice, pepper and a barely perceptible sense of oak.

Oaked Chardonnay –
A traditional varietal aged 12 months in fine crafted, American Oak barrels to allow the release of coffee, mocha, chestnuts and other traditional flavors unique to this grape.

Stone House Red –
A blend of Merlot, Cabernet Franc and Cabernet Sauvingnon.

Stone House White –
A marriage of classic chardonnay and crisp seyval blanc and vignols (Ravat 51). Flavors blend superbly during careful aging in primarily stainless steel and some oak.

Merlot –
A deep purple colored wine with complex aromas and a touch of spiciness and blackberry.

Cayuga –
A white wine with a crisp finish and a touch of citrus.

Seyval Blanc –
A crispy white wine with a hint of fruit.

Hopkins Vineyard

Hopkins Vineyard
25 Hopkins Road
New Preston, CT 06777
(860) 868-7954
www.HopkinsVineyard.com

Set on the northern shore of Lake Waramaug, Hopkins Vineyard, a family-owned Connecticut Century Farm, proudly maintains a tradition of making fine wines of award-winning quality. In 1787, Elijah Hopkins, returning from the Revolutionary War, chose this rich and fertile site on Lake Waramaug to settle his family and start the Hopkins Farm. Our farm has witnessed many diversified forms of agriculture over the years including the raising of sheep, race horses, grain crops, tobacco, and in the more recent past dairy farming. In 1979, the first vines were planted and our 19th century barn was converted into a state-of-the-art winery.

"My Chardonnay will surprise you. Sure, you know California and French wines. But you may not have had the experience of tasting a glass of Hopkins Chardonnay. We grow our grapes and produce our wines with care, right here at Hopkins Vineyard in the hills of Litchfield, Connecticut. Come visit us and taste our wines. Our friendly and knowledgeable staff will guide you with your wine selections. Sample the many wines we offer and hear an explanation of the ingredients, winemaking techniques and suggestions for food accompaniments. Once you have tried them all, enjoy a glass of your favorite wine in Connecticut's first winery-established wine bar. We're a lot closer to France and California than you might think."

Bill Hopkins, Winemaker
Hilary Hopkins, President

Welcome to one of Connecticut's premier vineyards. Hopkins Vineyard has been making wine in Connecticut for over 25 years. Located in the scenic Litchfield Hills, we produce over eleven different varieties of award winning wines. Come visit us in one of the most scenic areas of Connecticut.

Sparkling Wine - Gold Label –

Estate Bottled - A traditional méthode champenoise blend of barrel-aged Chardonnay and Pinot Noir with layers of creamy, buttery, nutty fruit and a fabulously crisp finish. Food pairings: Almost everything tastes better with bubbly! All-time favorites are lobster, shrimp, scallops and crab, however the preparation.

Vineyard Reserve –

2006 Estate Bottled - Made from our estate-grown Seyval and Vidal Blanc grapes, Vineyard Reserve is stylistically similar to Viognier, with its crisp, dry, blossom- and stone-fruit aromas. This wine has a natural affinity for Asian and Indian foods. Food pairings: Curried mussels, chicken Vindaloo, sesame noodles with baby greens and cucumbers, sushi or ginger shrimp with basmati rice.

Red Barn Red –

A medium-bodied, dry red. This wine offers a splendid bouquet and black currant overtones. Marvelous with roast lamb, steaks and chops or hearty pasta dishes.

Cabernet Franc –

2003 Estate Bottled - Hopkins Cabernet Franc is entirely estate-grown and is truly at its best in the climate of Litchfield County, with its sunny days and cool evenings. This full-bodied red is full of tannin; rich, concentrated black currant; dried fig; spice; and earthiness. Food pairings: Grilled lamb chops with mint; tomato and onion relish; braised short ribs with creamy polenta; grilled, marinated flank steak with veggies and blue cheese; or a nice, hot bowl of French onion soup.

Westwind –

2006 Estate Bottled - This white, semi-sweet, picnic-style wine is light and very crisp with a floral, fruity finish. Food pairings: Endive with lobster salad, honey and thyme-grilled peaches with proscuitto, turkey Waldorf salad with dried apricots and chêvre dressing, or chicken salad wraps.

Sachem's Picnic –

Sachem's Picnic is a semi-sweet, low-tannin wine, light in color with bright raspberry, blackberry, and plum fruit. It is best enjoyed within a year or two. Food pairings: Picnic basket fried chicken, Carolina pulled pork sandwiches, a classic burger with the "works" or a good dog (we like ours with caramelized onions and mustard).

Vidal Blanc 2006 –

Estate Bottled - This late-harvest dessert wine is luscious and nectar-sweet with wonderful flavors of orchard fruit and hazelnuts. Food pairings: Grilled, rum-marinated ripe pineapple with rum raisin ice cream; Maine blueberry pie; or simple lemon bars.

Ice Wine 2006 –

Estate Bottled - the traditional way. It shows harmonious, ripe fruit flavors of apple, peach preserve, and apricot. Perfectly sweet with well-balanced acidity. Food pairings: Peach and plum crostada, French apple tart, crême brulée, or simple sugar cookies.

Jerram Winery

Jerram Winery
535 Town Hill Road (Route 219)
New Hartford, CT 06057
(860) 379-8749
www.JerramWinery.com

Jerram Winery is one of Connecticut's newer farm wineries. It is located in the historic Town Hill section of New Hartford, the site of the original town settlement dating to the early 1700's. Because of the elevation, the vineyards enjoy a relatively long growing season that enables the vines to produce well-matured grapes necessary for the production of high quality wines.

The winery is run by James Jerram. He has extensive experience in the food and beverage industries, including wines and spirits. He holds a B.S. in Agriculture from Rutgers University in New Jersey, and an advance degree in Operations Management from Rensselear Polytechnic Institute. His interest in wine making was stimulated by Dr. Konstantine Frank of New York and Dr. Carlos Aggazotti of California.

Farm wineries began years ago as a way to supplement the farmer's income. Most were extremely modest undertakings. Today, farm wineries provide an added dimension for those who enjoy wine. Visiting a vineyard during the growing season is a wonderful way to see Nature working her miracles. Visiting a winery provides the opportunity to see how wine is made and, and at Jerram Winery, taste the different wines while chatting with the winemaker about his wine making philosophy. Thanks for letting us serve you and – SALUT!

Our tasting room allows us the luxury of accommodating more patrons at the wine bar, the ability to host social, business, and opening receptions for very talented artists who display their works in our art gallery. Jerram Winery offers private wine tastings and special events (indoor or under a tent) for groups of 10 to 60 people.

Vespers –
Introduced in 2005, it is a very sweet wine made from Vignole grapes. Ultra-smooth in the style of a late-harvest dessert wine...but it can be wonderful any time. Cheese and dessert wines find successful companionship, so pair it with a cheese or two before dinner, or as a dessert.

Nor'Easter –
Another new wine (December 2004), Nor'Easter is appropriately named for this part of the country. A real table 'wind' blended from two varieties of grapes. It is a semi-sweet wine that is smooth, satisfying, and finishes with a hint of raspberry.

Aurora –
A white table wine, is also new at the winery (Fall 2004). It is blended from two grape varieties that results in a smooth, fruity, and moderately sweet wine. Try this wine with spicy foods, especially Tex Mex cuisine. It also pairs well with an aged goat chees. Also with brie/mango quesadillas topped with a lime and sour cream.

Gentle Sheperd –
A unique blend of Aurore (a French hybrid) and other fine grape varieties. Fruity, slightly sweet, and refreshing, serve as an aperitif or with fish, pasta, or other casual fare. Serve chilled.

Seyval Blanc –
A crisp, dry white wine that can enhance any occasion. Serve it with cheese and crackers, with hors d' oeuvres, or with meals featuring fish or poultry. Serve chilled.

White Frost –
A light and delicate wine made with superior quality Chardonnay grapes. With a hint of oak in the background, this is a wine to consider as an aperitif or with meals featuring veal, poultry, or oriental cuisine. Serve only slightly chilled.

S'il Vous Plait –
A light bodied red wine with herbal tones and earthy origins. Made from Cabernet Franc grapes, this wine is an excellent choice to serve with lighter fare such as pasta, a chef's salad, or even pizza!

Highland Reserve –
A blend of fine red wines that are aged until ready for bottling. This is a wine that can be served with meals as diverse as casual lunches to formal dining occasions.

Marachel Foch –
This red wine is produced from the French hybrid Foch vine. It is a dry and robust, medium bodied wine that is well suited to accompany cheese and crackers, luncheons, or formal dinners.

Our Sweet Rose –
The newest wine at the winery. A slightly sweet rose style wine, with a cherry character.

Jonathan Edwards Winery

Jonathan Edwards Winery
74 Chester Maine Road
North Stonington, CT 06359
(860) 535-0202
www.JEdwardsWinery.com

Located in the quaint town of North Stonington, Jonathan Edwards Winery is situated on a beautiful 48-acre hilltop overlooking the Atlantic Ocean. The Edwards family has taken a unique approach to providing you with the best wine tasting experience possible. Jonathan Edwards handcrafts both premium Napa Valley, California and estate Connecticut wines to highlight each coasts unique climate. The two diverse product lines complement each other and allow our guests to sample delicious wines that showcase what each area is known for.

We welcome you to come visit our classic New England style, state-of-the-art winery for a personalized experience in a warm, relaxing atmosphere. We want visitors to be able to share part of their day with us; taste our wines, take a tour of our winery and vineyards, enjoy a picnic, and browse our gift shop for wine related items and special local treats. Each season has its own unique charm, and we encourage you to visit whenever you can steal some time for yourself, with your family, or as a romantic retreat.

Upon purchasing the winery, previously called Crosswoods Vineyards, all of the vineyards had to be removed due to years of neglect. As sad as that may seem, it provided an excellent opportunity to start fresh and utilize the latest technology in our vineyards. Located nine miles from the coast, our site provides us with moderating temperatures from the Long Island Sound which extends the fall season for optimal grape maturation. Being perched on the South side of a hill allows for full sun exposure for our grapes and excellent airflow to dry off our vines after a summertime shower. Additionally, an extensive drainage system known as "tiling" has been installed throughout our vineyards. Every vineyard row now has a drainage tile to allow excess water to drain down and out of the vineyard, allowing warmer soils in the spring, increased aeration in the soil, and prevention of excess moisture in the winter. Our vineyard is the only fully "tiled" vineyard in New England and we believe this gives our site a distinct advantage. Vineyard manager, Jon Edwards, devotes all his time and energy into making sure that each vine gets the individual hands-on attention that ultimately leads to healthy, balanced, premium vines. We at the Jonathan Edwards Winery believe that fine wine is truly created in the vineyard.

Aside from the spectacular panoramic views including distant views of the Connecticut shoreline, our winery situated on nearly 50 pastoral acres truly maintains the vintage New England character. Complete with a stone fireplace and custom built wine bar, our tasting room evokes the mixed spirit of Napa Valley within elegant Connecticut farm country. Our friendly and educated tasting room staff is here to welcome each visitor and guide you through your tasting as well as answer any questions you may have. Picnics are always welcome or choose from our a la carte menu of baguettes, locally made cheeses,   olives, and dipping oils to accompany a glass of wine. Whether you are a couple on a weekend getaway, or a serious wine connoisseur out to enjoy intricate wines, you are sure to enjoy yourself!

Jonathan Edwards Winery is quickly gaining a reputation for creating premium quality Napa Valley wines. While living in Napa Valley, winemaker Jonathan Edwards carefully selected grapes from specific vineyards each chosen to enhance the grapes varietal characteristics. These vineyards were then placed under long term contracts with our winery which ensures product consistency. During harvest season our grapes are hand picked under our direct supervision, and then immediately begin their transition into wine in California. Jonathan does this to maintain optimal freshness and stability of our premium wines. The young wine is then brought to Connecticut in refrigerated trucks to begin 12-18 months of barrel aging and bottling. This allows us to bring the best the West Coast has to offer to your doorstep. Jonathan Edwards Winery currently features Napa Valley Chardonnay, Merlot, Zinfandel, Cabernet Sauvignon, Syrah, and Petite Sirah. We also offer a Zinfandel Port and Syrah Port. These ports can only be purchased at the winery as production is limited. We also offer a full line of premium estate Connecticut wines. Jonathan has selected varietals that highlight our unique New England coastal climate. These grapes are harvested from our vineyards by hand, often by our own customers! Traditional fruit forward flavors are to be expected. Our estate wines currently include Chardonnay, Gewürztraminer, and Cabernet Franc. We will also have a Riesling and Pinot Gris as our vineyards come into production.

2006 Estate Connecticut Chardonnay –
One of our customer and staff favorites! Enjoy the ultra bright, fruit forward citrus bouquet of green apples and lemons, which is framed with light nuances of smoky vanilla oak from our large French barrels. This silky smooth, easy drinking wine pairs perfectly with seafood and fresh cheeses or is excellent all by itself on a lazy Sunday afternoon.

2005 Estate Connecticut Cabernet Franc –
The first release of our Estate grown red wine. One year of barrel aging highlights the cherry, blackberry fruit flavors and adds some vanilla highlights but keeps the tannins on the finish soft. Drink now or age for 3-5 years.

2005 Napa Valley Chardonnay –
This vintage continues in our tradition of super complex, highly drinkable Napa Chardonnays. Beginning with an aroma of ripe apricots and pears, this full-bodied wine finishes with soft flavors of light caramel. Pasta dishes and poultry are perfect accompaniments.

2004 Napa Valley Merlot –
Our 2004 offering is sourced from a thirty-five year old vineyard on the south side of Calistoga. Older vineyards often produce more robust wines, as evident in this Merlot. A gorgeous dark ruby color is pleasing to the eye and the deep black cherry aroma paired with a long complex finish will thrill your other senses as well. This bold Merlot will continue to develop in the bottle for at least 5-8 years. Enjoy this with red pasta dishes, almost any meats and alongside your favorite cheeses.

2004 Napa Valley Cabernet Sauvignon –
A long slow harvest season resulted in the picking of our Cabernet grapes on October 30th revealing soft tannins and subtle aromatic nuances. Earthy tones of tobacco, dark chocolate and peat continue to dominate the bouquet of our 2004 Cabernet Sauvignon.

2003 Napa Valley Syrah –
Extended barrel aging for over 2 years enriches our Yountville Syrah to its fullest potential. Upfront dark cherry aromas transition into dark chocolate and black raspberry on the palate. Our bold Syrah is sure to please now, or improve over the next 8-10 years.

145

Jones Winery

Jones Winery
606 Walnut Tree Hill Road
Shelton, CT 06484
(203) 929-8425
www.JonesFamilyFarms.com

For over one hundred and fifty years, six generations of the Jones family have farmed their land in the White Hills of Shelton, Connecticut. The Jones Winery continues the family's tradition of growing high quality crops that celebrate the great bounty of local farmlands. The farm's vineyard and famous berry harvests allow the winery to create a wonderful selection of traditional grape wines and specialty fruit wines.

Jamie Jones, the sixth generation of Jones farmers, planted the beginnings of his vineyard in 1999 and continues to expand the vineyard each year. A farmer all his life, Jamie tends to his grapes with much care, knowing that great wines can only come from a great vineyard. The vineyard includes European vinifera such as Cabernet Franc, Merlot, Lemberger and Pinot Gris. American hybrid varieties, such as Seyval Blanc and Cayuga White, also thrive. With his fruit wines, Jamie creates wines that showcase the wonderful taste and aromas of his farm's delicious, sun-ripened berries.

With the family's rich farming history and dedication to Connecticut agriculture, the winery places a strong emphasis on utilizing local fruit from the Jones vineyards and fields as well as from other outstanding Connecticut growers. For those interested in tasting the true local terroir, the Jones Winery is the place to visit.

The Tasting Room is located in a historic 19th century dairy barn. From May through November, the Tasting Room is open Friday, Saturday and Sunday from 11:00 AM to 5:00 PM. During the Christmas season, the winery is open seven days a week for wine sales and offers wine tastings only on weekday afternoons.

The Jones Winery always garners rave reviews for its knowledgeable, friendly staff and its relaxed, enjoyable atmosphere. Guests leave the Tasting Room enthusiastic about Jones Wines, eager to return to the Tasting Room and the farm, and excited about supporting Connecticut agriculture.

The Jones Winery is located at the heart of a beautiful 400-acre farm. When visiting the winery, people can also harvest seasonal crops at the Jones Family Farms – the finest and freshest strawberries, blueberries, pumpkins, squashes and Christmas trees.

VINTNER'S SELECT ESTATE WINES

Cabernet Franc – A blend of Cabernet Franc and Merlot from the Jones Winery's Pumpkinseed Hill vineyard, this wine is aged in American oak barrels for over one year.

Pinot Gris – Created from Pinot Gris grapes from the Jones Winery's Pumpkinseed Hill vineyard, this full bodied, dry white wine has rich taste typical of Pinot Gris from Alsace.

PREMIUM TABLE WINES

Ripton Red – A dry, medium-bodied red wine in the European Rosso style, Ripton Red complements many types of meals and events, from hearty pasta dishes to grilled meats.

Stonewall White – This dry, crisp white wine has fruity hints of green apple and citrus. With its clean finish, it can be elegantly paired with a great variety of foods, especially seafood.

Woodlands White – A refreshingly crisp wine with a delicately sweet finish, Woodlands White is the winery's most popular white wine.

Dawn's First Blush – This pleasingly sweet blush wine has clean finish, making it a perfect wine for summer gatherings. Created from a blend of Connecticut apples, pears and black currants, the wine has a wonderful fruity aroma. It complements many types of Asian cuisine including spicy dishes.

Harvest Time – This apple and pear wine is delicately sweet with crisp fruit flavors. It is perfect for holiday meals, such as those featuring roasted turkey or roast pork.

Strawberry Serenade – A sparkling wine created from the Jones farm's delicious strawberries. It combines the fun of having strawberries with champagne! Lightly sweet and bubbly, it is a great wine for brunches, parties and special occasions.

DESSERT WINES

Raspberry Rhapsody – Sweet and bursting with raspberry flavor, their very popular, award-winning wine can be enjoyed as an aperitif or with desserts.

Black Currant Bouquet – This full bodied wine, with its robust berry taste, finishes with a smooth sweetness. This award-winning wine can be paired with luscious treats, such as dark chocolate.

Strawberry Splendor – Our sun-ripened strawberries, harvested from the Jones farm's famous strawberry fields, create a wonderful wine that captures the distinctive taste and aroma of the strawberry.

Please note, the above list is a selection of Jones Winery wines. Since the wines are all handcrafted, each year there are changes to wine list. For the current wine list, please visit the winery's website at www.JonesFamilyFarms.com.

Land of Nod

The Land of Nod Winery
99 Lower Road
East Canaan, CT 08062
(860) 824-5225
www.LandofNodWinery.com

The Land of Nod Vineyard and Winery is located in Litchfield County, situated in the foothills of the Berkshires, on land steeped in early American History. The Land of Nod vineyard continues the

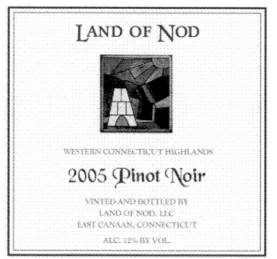

American tradition of skill and excellence in craftsmanship. The farm has been designated a Connecticut "Farm of Distinction" as a nationally recognized Bicentennial Farm and has been in continuous ownership by the same family for more than 200 years. We believe that wine is food from the land, and is at its best when served with food.

Our complimentary tasting room is open on Fridays, Saturdays, and Sundays April 1 – October 31 and by appointment.

In addition to wine, we offer a wide selection of maple syrup products, jams, jellies, pickles and magnificent yarns from our own sheep.

Bus tours and groups are welcomed but we would appreciate a call or email ahead of time so we may properly accommodate your visit. Please give us a call to schedule wine delivery or email us at info@landofnodwinery.com.

The Vineyard: Many of the grapevines are planted on the same fields where local iron industry companies produced tools and implements used by the Colonial army during the American Revolution. At present, the vineyard is planted with approximately 10 acres of Bianca, Pinot Noir, Cabernet Franc, Malbec and Chardonnay grapes.

The vineyard's neighborhood bustles with activity, including hiking, skiing and picnicking. Maple syrup is produced from February through March and sold in the sugarhouse and in the winery shop. Be sure to stop by the Beckley Furnace just up the road from the winery. The Beckley Iron Furnace is Connecticut's best preserved example of a technology that has long since vanished and is part of the National Register of Historic Places.

We appreciate your business and would love to hear from you.

Come and enjoy! Connect with the simple beauty of this bicentennial farm that the Adam Family has owned and farmed for over eight generations. While you are in the neighborhood explore the over 600 acres of state recreational forest.

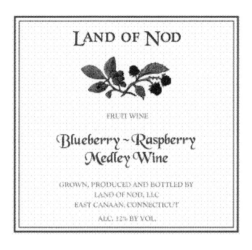

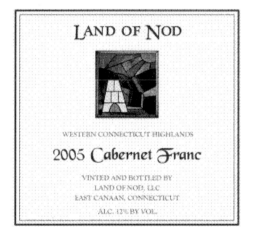

THE LAND OF NOD

"Wine is food from the land... More than any other food, wine embodies the elements of the place it was produced"

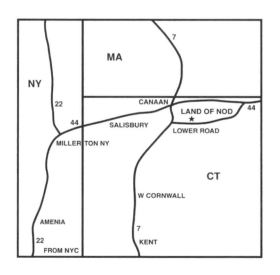

149

McLaughlin Vineyards

McLaughlin Vineyards
14 Albert's Hill Road
Sandy Hook, CT 06482
(866) 599-9463 or (203) 426-1533
www.McLaughlinVineyards.com

McLaughlin Vineyards is a year-round farm dedicated to the production of quality wines and maple syrup in a natural environment. Located in Southern Connecticut, the 160 acre historic operation includes 15 acres of vineyards, a 2500 case winery, hiking trails, wine education seminars, a sugar house, sugar maple trees, and even a 50 acre wildlife and bald eagle sanctuary. Hour hours are 11:00 to 5:00 everyday during the summer. November to May we are open 11:00 to 5:00 Wednesday thru Sunday and Monday & Tuesday by appointment. Please contact us for up to the minute information.

Have you been looking for an intimate and unique site to host a get-together for co-workers or friends? Our tasting room is available daily 5:00 to 9:00 pm. for private wine tastings and parties up to 40. Have a casual evening of wine and hors d'oeuvres or host a more formal "how to" wine tasting program. For details please see our website. McLaughlin also hosts many unique programs throughout the year: jazz afternoons, cooking demos, wine tasting seminars, bald eagle viewing and lunch, winery tours, and seasonal open houses. Give a gift certificate to teachers, babysitters, friends, and family and let them choose their perfect outing. Gift giving doesn't get any easier than this!

This holiday season we are pleased to announce our newest offering "The Wine Club." Give the gift of wine that keeps on giving. Many of our customers love to give our wines for the holidays or special occasions. Our products are made in limited quantities and are hand-produced in Connecticut. This unique program automatically sends 2 bottles of our Wine of the Month 3, 6, or 12 times a year. We provide recipes and tasting notes with each shipment. When new wines or vintages are released, "The Wine Club" participants are the first customers to receive them.

Partial list of our wines, please check our website for an up-to-date list:

Snow Goose –
This sweet white is a special blend of 100% estate-grown Connecticut grapes. Our family is dedicated to producing quality wines in a natural and historic setting. Come explore our farm this winter and perhaps catch a glimpse of the snow goose flying high over the vineyards.

Coyote Blue –
Our most popular white wine is semi-sweet, refreshing, and clean. It is bottled in the striking cobalt blue bottle. Made from estate-grown grapes this wine is sure to please those who prefer fruity wines.

Vista Muse –
A clean, dry blend of Chardonnay and the most widely grown white-grape in the Northeast, Seyval Blanc. 50% of each varietal yields a wine that pairs wonderfully with seafood and chicken.

Vista Reposa –
A very nice dry and fruity wine made from Connecticut-grown Cabernet Franc. Barrel aged in American oak gives the wine structure but remaining well-balanced.

Merlot –
Our most popular red is smooth, elegant, and dry.

Maple Syrup is produced from sap collected from sugar maple trees during late winter. The season in Connecticut ranges from early February through the third week in March with weather the determining factor. Ideal sugaring weather is 40 degree days and freezing nights. The sap is taken to the sugar house where it is boiled down to maple syrup. Pure maple syrup has nothing added! All of our syrup is bottled at our sugar house. Our 100% pure maple syrup comes in a variety of containers.

Grade A – Dark Amber –
Our 100% pure maple syrup comes in a variety of containers and is bottled at our sugar house.

Miranda Vineyard

Miranda Vineyard
42 Ives Road
Goshen, CT 06756
(860) 491-9906
www.MirandaVineyard.com

Welcome to Miranda Vineyard. Below you will find descriptions of our delicious wines and information about our family. Please enjoy your visit.

Some sons learn how to fish from their fathers. Others learn how to play baseball. Manny Miranda learned how to make wine. As far back as he can remember, when summer turned to fall, he and his father and grandfather would be busy for days in the courtyard of the family house, crushing grapes, squeezing them in a hand press and fermenting the grapes into wine. Over the years, Manny learned from his father and grandfather, in the same way they had learned from their fathers and grandfathers before them. He learned how to blend wine, to age it, perfect it, and, of course enjoy it.

Since he was a small boy growing up in Portugal, Manny dreamed of planting his own vineyard and building his own winery. It took more than 50 years, but he and Maria finally did it.

Recently they both retired, Manny from his own construction company, Maria as a school principal. And now they're doing the opposite of what many retired couples would do. They're starting all over again. They've been busy perfecting those old world

traditions Manny had passed down to him and they've created some very special wines they hope you enjoy as much as they do. Cheers! Or as they say in Portuguese – Saude!

Jeremy River Whit
A semi-sweet blend
our blends. Great w
2006 International E

Salmon River Whit
A barrel fermented c
citrus with soft oak.
Amenti Del Vino Int

Blackledge White –
A full bodied, dry w
Eastern Wine Compe

Barrel Select Chard
A rich, full of fruit cl
apple on the palate, t
New England seafc
Competition.

Riesling –
A classic crisp, Alsat
with pink grapefruit,
delicate seafoods, c
Competition.

Gewurztraminer –
A beautiful off-dry w
of fruit at start on the
pear and a crisp, mine
ham, pork, chicken, sc
Amenti Del Vino-East

St. Croix –
Aged 10 months, our
the palate with a finish
as well as grilled salmc

Salmon River Red –
A lighter red blend, ba
2003 International Ea
Commercial Wine Con

Cayuga –
A very crisp, dry, full c
apple and crisp pear. Br

Westchester Red –
A semi-sweet red blenc
raspberry and blackberı
with spicy, hearty dish
2002 Amenti Del Vino

Woodridge White –
A versatile New England wine, blending chardonnay and seyval blanc grapes. Refreshing for a summer afternoon and complicated enough for an evening dinner party.

Rosé –
A delightful honey bouquet exposing hints of cherries, strawberries, and watermelon. Delightful to the palate. Pairs well with cold hors d'oeuvres or fruit.

Merlot –
A dry complex wine with nuances of licorice and berries. Aged in French oak. Excellent choice with pasta, roasts, or steaks. Decadent with chocolate.

Seyval Blanc –
A refreshing, light and fruity crisp white wine. Compliments the flavor of poultry and is excellent with seafood. Serve chilled.

Chardonnay –
A sophisticated, full-bodied wine. A floral bouquet of apricot and peach, with hints of butternut and nutmeg. Perfect to serve with fish or poultry.

Sharpe Hill Vineyard

Sharpe Hill Vineyard
108 Wade Road
Pomfret, CT 06258
(860) 974-3549
www.SharpeHill.com

Priam Vineya[...]
historic town of [...]

The winery was b[...]
as a New Englan[...]
make use of the l[...]
well as the use of[...]
tanks, to help r[...]
environmentalists,[...]
propagating blueb[...]
a healthy vineyard[...]
which are release[...]
grapes are hand p[...]
flavor, which ul[...]

Come and visit Sharpe Hill Vineyard, the award winning winery of Connecticut's Quiet Corner! Sharpe Hill Vineyard has received over 225 medals in international tastings and is located in the town of Pomfret - just minutes from scenic Route 169 and from the Putnam Antiques District.

Although growing grapes in northeastern Connecticut provides us with the challenge of harsh winter weather, our vineyard (which is situated on a 700 foot slope) provides us with a microclimate that mimics many of the wine regions of Europe. In fact, our latitudinal location is comparable to that of Rome, Italy. Our vineyard's microclimate affords us the luxury of growing such vinifera grapes as Chardonnay and Cabernet Franc. We planted our first grapevines in 1992. The vineyard has now expanded to 25 acres which include plantings of Chardonnay, Melon de Bourgogne and Vignoles for white wines; and Cabernet Franc, Carmine and St. Criox for red wine. We are continuing our vineyard expansion program with plantings of Riesling, Dornfelder, Gamay, and Landot Noir which will begin to produce crops with the 2007 vintage.

Our tasting room is open year round for tasting and the purchase of wine and wine related products, including gift certificates, every Friday, Saturday, and Sunday, from 11:00 a.m. to 5:00 p.m. Reservations for a tasting are not required, please visit anytime during business hours. There are no tours at this time, however you may take a self guided walk into the vineyard and enjoy the spectacular view

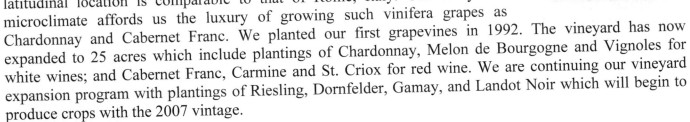

at the top, which overlooks a portion of Connecticut, Massachusetts and Rhode Island. We hope you'll join us in the near future, and we look forward to offering you a sample of what we consider to be some of the finest wines vinted.

The ' Ou
overl sta
produ up
a wi En
Franc hav
produ wir
sorte thro
perfo
Stoni
Eac
In lat the
for th abo
hand If y
outsta mo
ferme

The (Son

In the
acros 200
releas Thi
contir add
excel also
barrel cuis
chard
with 1

Sea
This
Cayl
The (grea

2003
traditi
caber
blend
succe

Ballet of Angels –
A crisp and semi-dry white wine with a lovely floral bouquet. It has flavors of citrus and pear with a long finish. We suggest serving this wine well chilled as an aperitif or with spicy foods. Ballet of Angels has received 71 medals!

Sharpe Hill Vineyard American Chardonnay –
A light, crisp Chardonnay with a hint of lime and touch of oak. Our American barrel fermented Chardonnay is best served with light fare. American Chardonnay has received 44 medals.

Sharpe Hill Vineyard Reserve Chardonnay –
An estate bottled, Burgundian Chardonnay. This elegant dry wine is both crisp and well balanced, and has a soft finish. It also complements food very well - especially seafood and chicken. Reserve Chardonnay has received 13 medals.

Red Seraph –
A dry red table wine featuring a robust blend of Merlot and St. Croix. This exquisitely colored ruby red wine is soft and smooth, the perfect accompaniment to beef, lamb and pasta dishes. Red Seraph has received 17 medals.

St. Croix –
A Rhone style red wine made completely from estate grown, hand picked St. Croix grapes aged in oak barrels for over 18 months. The St. Croix is unique and elegantly dry with a smooth buttery finish, a perfect accompaniment to beef, lamb, and pasta dishes. St. Croix has received 17 medals.

Cabernet Franc –
A Bordeaux style wine that is made entirely from Cabernet Franc grapes. This wine has a classic Cabernet bouquet and a delicate soft finish. We suggest serving this wine with all red meat dishes as well as chocolate desserts. Cabernet Franc has received 19 medals.

Select Late Harvest –
A wine that is made entirely from estate grown, handpicked botrytised Vingnoles. This wine is a mouth filling blend of honey and fruit, with a nicely balanced level of acidity, and a bouquet of peaches and apricots as well as a remarkably long finish. Select Late Harvest has received 32 medals.

Sharpe Hill Dry Riesling –
A fragrant, dry Alsatian style Riesling that offers a gentle, floral bouquet coupled with hints of lemon zest and sweet grapefruit on the tongue. The first vintage was released October 2004. Our Dry Riesling has received 6 medals.

Cuvee Ammi Phillips –
Our limited edition Cuvee is made completely in brand new French Oak barrels with Chardonnay grapes from North Fork, Long Island. This full bodied Chardonnay is best when served with salmon/seafood or poultry dishes. Released summer of 2006. The Cuvee Ammi Phillips Chardonnay has received 5 medals in Competitions and has received the highest score for a New England wine by Wine Spectator magazine.

Dry Summer Rose –
Released summertime 2006 our dry Rose is beautifully colored and aromatic with hints of strawberry. This wine has received 4 medals in International Competitions.

Taylor Brooke Winery

Taylor Brooke Winery
848 Rte. 171
Woodstock, CT 06281
(860) 974-1263
www.TaylorBrookeWinery.com

Welcome to Taylor Brooke Winery. Here, tucked in the scenic rolling hills of northeastern Connecticut, we tend to over 2,000 carefully cultivated vines and create our wines to reflect the sense of living…strong roots, a tender touch, caring manner, nurturing environment, and a commitment to quality. It's a philosophy that worked for our family; it's working for our wines.

Taylor Brooke Winery produces a premium line of high quality vinifera and specialty wines. These wines have been developed by the winemaker/owner, Dick Auger, in a very unique way; involving friends and family to taste and comment on the wines during development. This broad spectrum of palates helped create wines that appeal to a wide variety of wine drinkers; from the novice to the connoisseur. The wines are produced from our own grapes as well as fruit and juices procured locally and nationally.

Our mission is to produce a variety of high quality wines produced from grapes grown on site and procured from local farms. We believe that agriculture is an import part of the community and by establishing this winery and associated vineyard we will be able to continue the tradition of farming. Our business philosophy is this: Create opportunities to partner with local businesses to help support each other and our community.

Richard (Dick) and Linda Auger are the owners of Taylor Brooke Winery. Dick is responsible for overall management of the vineyard, winery and wine making processes. He has many years experience in making small batch wines. A Certified Facility Manager, Dick knows the importance of process, sanitation and statistical process control. With 20 years experience in the biotech manufacturing (fermentation) and pharmaceutical industry (bio-processing) and 5 years of hospital management, Dick understands the need for fiscal control and attention to winemaking process control. Linda brings 25 years experience in Human Resources and 10 years experience in Retail to the management of the tasting room and administration of the winery.

162

Riesling – This clean, crisp, dry white wine is slightly fruity with flavorful hints of peach & apricots. With its floral aroma and bouquet of honey, it's a nice balance of fresh fruit and crisp acidity. This wine pairs well with Asian food.

Woodstock Hill White – This truly distinct wine made from estate grown Riesling, St. Pepin. Melody and Vignoles, has a fruit forward and clean, bone dry finish. Excellent paired with light seafood and pasta.

Traminette – The Traminette grape is a Cornell University cross between the Seyval and Gewurztraminer grapes. The dry, spicy characteristics of the Gewurztraminer grape are evident, with notes of pineapple and apricot on the palette.

Green Apple Riesling – We start with 100% dry Riesling and add a natural green apple essence which produces a wonderful balance of apple flavor with the slight acidity and firm character of the Riesling grape. Wonderful with baked ham, barbeque chicken or pork.

Autumn Raspberry – 100% Riesling with a natural raspberry essence. Another semi-sweet favorite which is wonderful with roast chicken with rosemary. Make a reduction sauce for your roast pork and serve with dinner!

Cranberry Riesling – We bring in almost a ton of cranberries, ferment them into wine and age the wine for 10-11 months before blending it with our Riesling wine. Tart and dry, this wine is a must for Thanksgiving! Perfect holiday hostess gift!

Cabernet Franc – The Cabernet Franc grape is the fruitier relation of the Cabernet Sauvignon grape. Less herbaceous with less tannin, the style is reminiscent of a light, dry Pinot Noir. Pair with a dense fish, turkey, light pasta or rare roast beef.

Roseland Red – A Bordeaux blend of Cabernet Sauvignon, Merlot and Cabernet Franc. This wine is fruity and peppery with a hint of Hungarian oak.

Woodstock Valley Red – 100% St. Croix grapes from our vineyard. Aged for 18 months, this wine has highlights of soft berries, balanced tannin and a touch of Hungarian oak.

Late Harvest Riesling – This special dessert wine enchants the nose with ripe apricot, peach and honey. Apricot and honey notes continue into the flavor spectrum, with nuances of pineapple unfolding across a rich, concentrated palate. A firm acid profile balances the wine's sweetness, yielding a deep, lingering finish. The result is this balanced, nectar-like wine, truly the essence of the Riesling grape.

Chocolate Essence – Chocolate infused Merlot port! Strong chocolate on the nose, the fruity complexity (raspberries and cherries) of the Merlot port on the palate and a long, chocolate finish. This truly special wine is "dessert in a glass."

Raspberry Rendezvous – Intensely aromatic, this 100% Raspberry port-style dessert wine will warm you to the tips of your toes. Pairs well with anything chocolate or your favorite cheese cake.

White Silo Farm & Winery

White Silo Farm & Winery
32 Rt. 37 East
Sherman, CT 06784
(860) 355-0271
www.WhiteSiloWinery.com

White Silo Farm and Winery is a small specialty winery. All of our wine is produced from our own farm grown fruit. Experience the charm of an earlier era by touring the old barn where the winery is located. Visit the fermentation, bottling, and corking rooms where the classical art of wine making has been preserved. Located in beautiful Sherman Connecticut, the farm is one mile from center of Sherman. You can't miss the big white silo!

The dairy farm is now a Pick-Your-Own berry farm. You can Pick-Your-Own (PYO) delicious raspberries & blackberries. Three different varieties of raspberries are available, red, golden and orange. Our Pick-Your-Own farm is in season September & October, every day from 10:00 am - 6:00 pm. Please check picking and weather conditions.

The winery also boasts an Art Gallery, featuring the work of many talented artists and crafts people. Check our 'Gallery/Events' page on our website for more information.

Dry Wines:

Rhubarb – Dry, crisp and light. Goes well with pasta, fish, veal, chicken.

Blackberry – Dry, full-bodied with a hint of blackberries. Goes well with pork, duck, meat

Raspberry – Dry, delicate raspberry aroma. Goes well with chicken, light pasta dishes, salads, cheeses.

Black Current – Full-bodied with a long finish. Goes well with hearty meals, meat, duck.

Dessert Wines:

Rhubarb – Very mellow and smooth, no bite.

Blackberry – Very fruity flavor.

Raspberry – Strong fruit flavor.

Cassis – Nice sipping wine. Black current martinis, mix with champagne (kir).

HOUSE SPECIALTY BLACKBERRY SANGRIA
A 50/50 mix of our Dry Rhubarb and Sweet Blackberry wines

Blacksmiths Winery

Blacksmiths Winery
967 Quaker Ridge Road
South Casco, ME 04077
(207) 655-3292
www.BlacksmithsWinery.com

Blacksmiths Winery is Maine's largest winery producing grape wines and the first winery in Maine recognized with silver and bronze medals for a grape wine in International Competitions. Blacksmiths is also the first winery in Maine to produce fortified wines, both port and blueberry. Of course, we also

make popular wines made from native Maine fruit, including Blueberry, Cranberry, Elderberry and Raspberry, providing a spectrum of flavors to suit almost any taste.

The winery was started in 1999 at the site of the South Casco blacksmith. William Watkins apprenticed as the South Casco blacksmith in his late teens. As the village smithy, he worked long hours and neighbors saw sparks from the forge well into the night. He was notorious as a demanding craftsman, even making his own nails, as he insisted machine-made nails were not good.

Blacksmiths Winery opened 160 years later at the same location. The tasting room is in the original house, the winery is housed in the refurbished barn and the blacksmith shop is still on site (awaiting restoration). The first year we produced 1000 cases of wine and have been growing ever since, investing in newer and better technology for the production of fine wines.

Come visit the original Watkins' home, barn and blacksmith shop. While you're here, be sure to sample our award winning wine. We like to think that each one continues the blacksmiths' spirit of craftsmanship. The Tasting Room and Winery are at Route 302 and Quaker Ridge Road, opposite Cry of the Loon Shops in South Casco Village. Visitors can sample the wines and tour the winery daily from 11:00 am to 5:00 pm. Please visit our website for more information.

OFF DRY WINES:

Blueberry – A sumptuous blend of native Maine blueberries and a crisp white wine. Dry and delightful. Bring home a taste of Maine. A perfect pairing for pork, chicken or turkey.

Vidal Blanc – A crisp white wine recommended for a summer afternoon in Maine. Both to be savored while they last. Flavors of fresh pear and peach, similar to Riesling, Vidal Blanc pairs nicely with seafood and dishes with Asian flavored sauces.

Commissure – An off-dry red wine similar to Pinot Noir with ripe fruit flavors of fresh strawberry and a spicy-cinnamon finish. A blend of Chambourcin and Leon Millot grapes.

DRY WHITE WINES:

Trillium – Blacksmiths original blend of Chardonnay, Vidal Blanc and Pinot Gris. Trillium is lightly oaked with fresh, zingy fruit flavors. It pairs well with lighter foods with rich zesty flavors.

Pinot Gris – Also called Pinot Grigio in Italy, has full flavors of rich peach and pear, and an exciting spicy quality and acidity in the mouth. Lovely with salads, appetizers and simply prepared fish and shellfish. Our Pinot Gris is very concentrated and rich

DRY RED WINES:

Sangiovese – Deep ruby color, ripe plum nose, firm structure with balanced tannin and fruit, and a long, rich finish that shows French oak, plum and black cherry. A "Super Tuscan" style blend with 91% Sangiovese and 9% Cabernet Sauvignon.

Syrah – Yakima Valley Syrah shows brambly fruit flavors of raspberry and blackberry, with rich spice and pepper notes on a monumentally structured finish.

Merlot – A fruit-forward style with flavors of blueberries, plums and especially cherries, with a lovely soft beguiling bouquet of rose blossoms and chocolate. Crisply structured with tight fruit, Fermented and aged for 19 months in small French oak barrels.

Cabernet Sauvignon – 100% Cabernet Sauvignon fermented and aged in new French Oak Barrels for over 3 years. An intense Cabernet with aromas of ripe red berries with red cherry and spice. Great depth and length of fruit in the mouth with vanilla, chocolate and smoke.

DESSERT WINES:

Roughshod – Get a grip. Made with Maine blueberries blended with brandy. A delightful Port-style wine especially delicious with fruit desserts and anything vanilla.

Casco Port – The Chambourcin grape provides the hearty fruit flavors, which are balanced by the smooth finish of the brandy. A ruby port to enjoy with cheese, chocolate or walnuts.

Sparkling Cranberry – Bright pink color, clear and clean with an elusive cranberry and citrus nose. The flavor is a balanced sweet and tart cranberry while the Vidal Blanc provides a crisp finish.

Shalom Orchard Organic Winery

Shalom Orchard
158 Eastbrook Road, Route 200
Franklin, ME 04634
(207) 565-2312
www.ShalomOrchard.com

Shalom Orchard is located high on a ridge with beautiful views surrounding the farm. To the east the sun rises over our East Orchard and the Schoodic Mountains; to the south stretches Frenchman's Bay and the mountains of Mount Desert; to the west, the sun sets behind our West Orchard and the hills of Dedham & Bangor. We are located about 35 minutes from Bar Harbor and the Nova Scotia ferry, within sight are several beautiful lakes to enjoy water recreation and fishing. Nearby enjoy our lovely woods, or trails to hike the Schoodic Mountains. In the winter, there are ponds for ice-skating, snowmobile trails nearby, and bountiful opportunities for cross-country skiing.

The farmhouse dates back to about 1840 and the farm has been farmed for as long as anyone can remember. An Episcopal minister gave the name, originally Shalom Farm, back in the 1960's. There is an old photograph of a painting on the barn of a rainbow and doves, the peace message of the era. When we found the farm, the old-timers in the community told us of the old name and we re-named it Shalom Orchard, to reflect the 1000+ apple orchard now established. We adopted the logo, "Peace with Nature" as this is our commitment through our organic farming practices.

We are a certified organic farm and everything we grow or produce is according to organic standards. We primarily grow organic fruit - apples, blueberries, cherries and raspberries - for our wines or for wholesale or retail sale from the farm. We also grow vegetables for retail sale through our CSA or from our farm store. We raise chickens for eggs and meat, and we raise registered Rambouillet sheep for wool and meat. We have for sale beautiful yarns, both handspun and organically mill-spun sport-weight, both in natural colors and plant-dyed, as well as tanned pelts and fleece. We are committed to educating about organic farming and welcome school groups and tours. We participate in the Maine Organic Farmers and Gardeners apprenticeship program. We love to share our enthusiasm for what we do.

We are a stepfamily of 17 years. There are four children: Charlotte's daughter, Kendall, and son, Ben are grown and married with children of their own. Jim's boys, Ric and Jacob, have grown up on the farm and have been willing (mostly) helpers in all aspects of farm work. They are now in the leaving home stage of their lives. Charlotte is the farm manager, overseeing the organization and planning of the farm work with the assistance of farm workers and apprentices. She is also a Licensed Marriage and Family Therapist, with a part-time private practice in nearby Ellsworth. She has farmed since the 1970's, and co-owned a commercial vineyard and winery in Connecticut in the 1980's. Her interests include spinning, knitting and photography. Jim is manager of the winery production and sales. He has made wines as a hobby for almost twenty years before becoming a commercial winemaker. He is also a builder of post and beam structures and a Macintosh computer guru, having spent many years as a computer systems network administrator before farming full-time. Jim enjoys contra-dancing, folk music, shape-note singing, and sailing.

In 2002, we established a commercial winery featuring fruit and honey wines, produced from our own and other local organic fruits. We specialize in apple, blueberry and cranberry wines and smaller productions of raspberry, kiwi, and honey mead wines. Our wines have been very well reviewed and are available from our winery or in selected wine shops and natural food stores in Maine.

Community Supported Agriculture (CSA) is a community of people centered around a farm. CSA shareholders give the farm financial support in advance of the season, and in return the farm provides a weekly share of produce during the growing season. CSA reconnects people to the land that sustains them and builds rewarding relationships between the farmers and shareholders. By joining a CSA, you can participate in preserving a local farm and help foster renewable farming practices that enrich the earth. Want more information about Community Supported Agriculture? We've added a "What Is Community Supported Agriculture (CSA)?" page to our website with some more definitions and links to other CSA resources.

Shalom Orchard is a small farm so we are only looking for 15 - 20 members to be part of our CSA. We welcome our CSA members as part of our farm family and encourage their participation in all activities. We offer a wide variety of organic vegetables as well as chicken, eggs, apples, blueberries, raspberries and cherries. In addition members will have opportunities to buy our other products direct from our farm store. If you are interested in finding out more drop us a line at our webpage. We offer $20 and $30 per week shares over a 12 week period. Each week we will contact you with a summary of what is available and you can customize your order by simply replying to that message. For more information about how Shalom Orchard is implementing CSA visit our 'News' section of our website where you can read copies of our weekly summary letters to our members and even check out a few recipes members have given us.

In 2004, we were licensed as a bed and breakfast. Farm stays offer an opportunity to experience farm life and explore our beautiful Maine coast and the many recreational activities close by. Guests can participate in the seasonal activities of the farm or just relax. In a separate wing of the house, we offer two bedrooms, one upstairs and one downstairs. Also, downstairs is a bath and kitchenette, that is available to guests for light cooking. We will prepare you a true farm breakfast, featuring our own eggs and fruits, accompanied by pancakes or breads made from Maine-grown organic grains and maple syrup. Our downstairs room is handicap-friendly. We welcome children and most pets. Rooms have cable TV and broadband Internet access.

Sweetgrass Farm Winery & Distillery

Sweetgrass Farm Winery & Distillery
347 Carroll Road
Union, ME 04862
(207) 785-3024
www.sweetgrasswinery.com
www.backrivergin.com

Sweetgrass Farm
WINERY & DISTILLERY

Sweetgrass Farm Winery and Distillery is Maine's only winery and distillery using Maine grown fruits to produce fine wines and distinctive spirits. Our wines include apple, cranberry, blueberry, and peach. The distilled spirits are hand crafted in old world tradition with a copper alembic still capturing the full flavors of our Back River Gin and fruit brandies. Learn about wine production from award-winning winemaker and owner on our farm preserving Union's rich farming tradition. Hike our trails and enjoy breathtaking panoramic views of the Medomak river valley. Sweetgrass Farm is a family run business firmly rooted in the community, supporting local sustainable agriculture, and donating 10% of profits to organizations which support families, children, and rural life.

Our wines show the distinctive characters provided by each fruit and encompass many styles. Our spirits include Calvados, an oak aged apple brandy, and our Back River Gin which has won critical acclaim with a "Highly Recommend" four star rating in F. Paul Pacult's Spirits Journal; "A gin that pushes the white spirit envelope in a way that's creative and sophisticated."

Sweetgrass Farm Winery and Distillery is owned and operated by husband and wife Keith and Constance Bodine. Keith's expertise in winemaking coupled with Constance's business sense, hard work, and a huge amount of creativity has catapulted this small hand crafted winery into the spotlight. Keith received his masters in winemaking from UC Davis in 1995 and has worked at wineries in Napa and as far away as China. He continues to be a sought after winery and distillery consultant. Constance's work experience is centered on mathematical modeling and operations research, having worked as a power broker and consultant for several years before she turned her interests to business management. The owner's three children keep busy shepherding sheep, helping in the winery, and creating wine label artwork.

Apple Wine –
Crisp, fruity, and unlike any apple wine you have ever had.

Bleujolais –
Made from Union grown wild Maine blueberries, this vibrant young wine bursts with flavor yet is amazingly smooth.

Cranberry Apple –
A tart red that bursts with flavor.

Peach –
The taste of summer!

Cranberry Smash –
A cranberry taste explosion!

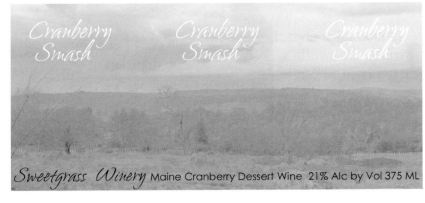

Back River Gin –
A smooth American style dry gin with a hint of spice and blueberries.

Pure Vanilla Extract –
Made from 100% organic Madagascar Bourbon Vanilla beans, 35% premium alcohol, and spring water, NO SUGAR added. Winemaker crafted for superior taste and quality. Fine vanilla, like wine, cannot be rushed. Deep vanilla flavor and aromas for all your homemade goods, just like grandma's. (6 oz. bottle)

181

Vintner's Cellar Winery

Vintner's Cellar Winery
1037 Forest Avenue
Portland, ME 04103
(207) 878-1119
www.MaineVintners.com

Please come join me at Vintner's Cellar Winery for a glass of vino!

I'm not stuffy, pretentious or elitist about wine. I believe that drinking wine should be an individual experience, enjoyed they way you want to enjoy it. I try very hard to make my customers feel at ease and comfortable at my winery. This is such a fun and unique way to learn about, taste and create wine.

Heidi Shangraw

Wine Parties

Schedule a Wine Making Party. If you know you want to make some wine simply call to set up a time for you and your friends to come in for a complimentary tasting. We will spend a few hours tasting various wines so you can choose one for your own. It's a fun way to discover a wine you love and share the experience with your friends. And if you decide to initiate a batch of your own, we can help you design a custom label for your wine bottles – which makes your wine perfect for gift-giving, weddings and anniversaries.

Your party can be as short as an hour or as long as three hours and generally consist of 4 to 24 guests or 6 to 12 couples. You can have the party catered, or if you wish, you can bring your own hors d'oeuvres. We kindly ask that you plan to design one batch of wine for every four people in attendance.

Vintner's Cellar will provide the tables, the space and - of course - the wine…

Discover Your Own Quality Wines

In just two short visits to Vintner's Cellar you can enjoy 24 bottles of your favorite wine - no grape stomping necessary. We start your batch in the store and then you come back in 6 to 8 weeks to pick up your wine.

We'll even help you design your own custom label. Imagine giving your own custom labeled wine as gifts to your clients – or serving your wine at your wedding, anniversary or company party.

Our table wines are available in Gold Medallion, Premium, and Supreme.
Wine prices include bottles, corks, shrinks and labels.

• Gold Medallion –
Made from the finest grape concentrates.
Ready for your enjoyment in as few as five weeks.
$175.00 for 24 750 ml. Bottles
$195.00 for 50 375 ml. Bottles

• Premium –
50/50 mixture of the best juice and concentrate produces a full-bodied and robust wine with excellent bouquet balanced with oak. (6 weeks)
$245.00 for 30 750 ml. Bottles
$265.00 for 60 375 ml. Bottles

• Supreme –
Made for the wine enthusiast. 100% pure juice harvested from the finest vineyards of the world. Produces an exquisite bouquet, body and nose. Should be well aged for perfection. (Allow 6-8 weeks)
$295.00 for 30 750 ml. Bottles
$315.00 for 60 375 ml. Bottles

Winterport Winery

Winterport Winery
279 South Main Street
Winterport, ME 04496
(207) 223-4500
www.WinterportWinery.com

The Winterport Winery is located in the historic village of Winterport, Maine, offering a selection of fruit wines, which capture the full essence of the fruit. These wines compliment various cuisines for formal or casual occasions.

The Winterport Winery, owned by Michael and Joan Anderson, opened its doors in the fall of 2001 but it really had its beginning in the Christmas gift of a home winemaking kit some 30 years earlier. What was a hobby then has now become a full time work and a family involved business - what used be stored in the family basement now occupies the 3200 sq. ft. winery and 1100 sq. ft. tasting room.

Our tasting room is a wonderful place to sample some of our wines. Come also to browse through our retail store and find that unique gift idea such as wine related items or something for that hard-to-shop for person. Come in and meet us. You might see some of the family here or some of our friends who are all part of Winterport Winery.

Blueberry Wines – DRY - 2006 Bronze Medal – The Big E; Cherry red color. Aromas of soft ripe fruit and well-integrated oak. DEMI - 2005 Double Gold Medal– IEWC and 2006 Bronze Medal at The Big E Starts sweet and finishes dry. The Dry pairs well with a homemade pasta topped with a marinara sauce while the Demi is a perfect accompaniment to steak, pheasant or venison.

Pear Wines – DRY - 2003 Bronze Medal Winner - American Wine Society. It is wonderfully smooth with a great mid-palette structure and a long finish. DEMI Pear is an amiable wine with deep aromas, bright fruit flavor and a smooth finish. Both are deliciously food friendly. Consider using the Dry Pear in place of the usual Chardonnay. The Demi is another fine sipping wine and pairs well with spicy foods.

Apple Wine – Our Apple Wine is fair colored and made from a variety of Maine apples. A delicious interplay between oak and fruit with a round, smooth body and a crisp dryness It is a refreshing apertif enjoyed by itself or when accompanied by aged cheeses.

Strawberry Wine – Our Strawberry Wine is delicate and soft to your palate with a very fruity nose. There's a hint of florals among the fruit. It's ever so lightly sweet with an enjoyable lingering flavor. Pairs well with light desserts.

Raspberry Rain – 2004 Bronze Award Winner - American Wine Society; Our Raspberry Rain has the mouth filling "jammy" flavor of raspberries sweetened to a dessert style. Raspberry Rain can be enjoyed by itself but is better with your favorite dessert, say, a luscious chocolate mousse or cheesecake.

Spring Fever – "You've never tasted apples and strawberries like this!" Winters are long in Maine - some say they're too long. So to celebrate spring now or anytime, we have created Spring Fever. This apple-strawberry blend is slightly dry, light and fruity with a kiss of sweetness. Spring Fever is reminiscent of an Alsatian Gewurztraminer or a German Riesling and pairs well with salads, hors d'oeuvres or light meals.

Orchard Blush – A fiery, ruby-red colored wine in the medium bodied rosé family. Orchard Blush is a blend of our Apple and Blueberry wines - a subtle combination of varietal fruit. Sure to please both red and white wine drinkers alike. Excellent chilled alone as a warm weather refreshment, pairs well with smoked meats or vegetarian dishes.

Cranberry Wine – 2004 Silver Award Winner - American Wine Society. Our Cranberry is a seasonal wine and can best be described as gently tart, but with a dry finish. Perfect with holiday meals and yet refreshing year-round.

The Flying Dutchman – 2003 Gold Medal Winner - American Wine Society; 2006 Silver Medal and highest ranking Maine wine at The Big E and 2007 Silver Medal at The Indy State Fair. The Flying Dutchman is a fortified blackberry wine finished in a port - style. It will delight you with its full fruit body and rich, lingering flavors. At the end of the meal you need nothing else.

Berry Chocolate – A dessert wine you will not want to share. This delicious wine starts with a blossoming of berry flavors followed by a velvety chocolate finish, a union to delight the palate, offering a balanced sweetness and a rich smoothness for your enjoyment. Luscious alone - alone with someone you love.

Massachusetts

Alfalfa Farm Winery

Alfalfa Farm Winery
267 Rowley Bridge Road
Topsfield, MA 01983
(978) 774-0014
www.AlfalfaFarmWinery.com

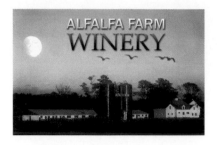

Come visit Alfalfa Farm Winery and taste what New England has to offer. A historic farm in the heart of Eastern Massachusetts, Alfalfa Farm mixes old-fashioned New England charm with the latest in winemaking technology. At our wine tastings, sample a variety of delicious wines, from dry Leon Millot to semi-sweet Aurora to a range of fruit wines. From traditional to fruit wines, dry to sweet, Alfalfa Farm serves up an abundance of delicious home-grown varieties.

Come visit us in the gift shop, open Saturdays and Sundays from 1:00 to 5:00 p.m. We sell a variety of home-grown wines, which you can sample in our store. While you're here, check out our wine-making operation and the following items and opportunities:

Picking parties: If you want to get your hands dirty -- and grape-stained -- come to one of our harvest parties. Cut bunches of ripe, luscious grapes right off the vines and help load them into the crusher. Sorry, we don't squish them with our bare feet! At the end of the day, pop a cork and enjoy the fruits of your labor.

Internships: Alfalfa Farm Winery is pleased to be able to offer an internship program for students interested in all aspects of winemaking: Care of the vines, harvesting, fermentation, etc.

Gift baskets: We custom-build gift baskets to suit our customers' needs. Load them up with your favorite wines, as well as crackers, bottle openers, glasses and other treats. Prices vary.

Crafts: Homemade arts, crafts and T-shirts are for sale in the gift shop.

Let Alfalfa Farm help you with your next function. Gather your friends, family or clients for a wine-tasting party. We will work with you to plan a party or business meeting in your home or office. We can help create a theme based on the food being served or the specific tastes of the host and guests. Our tastings generally have a party atmosphere with enough structure to keep them educational and enjoyable. If you prefer a more formal tasting, we can do that too. Our vineyard makes a beautiful backdrop for those wedding photos, and we have plenty of space to dance the night away. We can suggest caterers and musicians, too. For more information, please contact us. We're open on Saturdays and Sundays from 1:00 to 5:00 p.m., and Mondays from 3:00 to 5:00 p.m. by appointment to help our customers plan events at the winery including tastings. Check out our website for new wine-tasting packages. For your convenience, we now accept MasterCard and Visa. Hope to see you soon!

In recent years there has been an increasing interest in preserving historic and scenic landscapes in Massachusetts and around the country. This directly relates to conservation and open-space issues. Agriculture, like any business, depends on markets to be a productive landscape. One way farms in the U.S. have found to address these issues is through a business model called CSAs: Community Supported Agriculture. This is the practice of pre-selling 'shares" of the crop to consumers at the start of the growing season to be picked up by the share holders as the crop is harvested. Because wine grapes are a value-added crop, the process takes about a year from harvest to consumption. Alfalfa Farm Winery will be incorporating this process into its wholesale and retail marketing structure. We currently have an inventory of last year's wine to sell in this way. One share of any mixed varieties of wine in inventory is for sale for $150 per share. A share consists of one case of wine. People interested in Alfalfa Farm Winery's CSA can contact us.

Aurora –

A crisp white wine made from the aurora grape, one of the most widely planted varieties in the northeastern United States. The cool New England climate is perfect for early ripening. A semi-sweet wine with a rich, fruity flavor, aurora is a great alternative to a French Chablis and will complement any chicken or white pasta dish.

Cabernet Sauvignon –

Our easy drinking red! This medium-bodied red exhibits wonderful fruit flavors and low acid. Great for a table wine or to go with any meal.

Cranberry –

An Alfalfa Farm bestseller. Our cranberry is semidry with a full ruby color. It bursts with cranberry flavors right to the finish! Enjoy this wine as an aperitif, digestiv or all by itself. Best when mildly chilled.

Blueberry –

(semisweet or dry) An Alfalfa Farm classic. Made entirely from wild Maine blueberries, this wine comes in semisweet or dry versions with a smooth fruit finish. Can be enjoyed as a table wine or dessert wine.

Marechal Foch –

Our Marechal Foch is a semidry red wine with hints of strawberry and blackberry as well as a refreshing bite of tannin.

Merlot –

Our own version of one of the most popular varietals in the United States, our merlot is a medium-bodied dry red wine that goes well with red meats.

Seyval Blanc –

Always a winner! Seyval Blanc is a French-American hybrid grape that produces a medium-bodied white with honey aromas and grassy undertones. Great when chilled. Accompanies any white-meat dish.

Broad Hill Vineyards

Broad Hill Vineyards
583 Winter Street
Holliston, MA 01746
(508) 429-2891
www.BroadHill.com

Welcome to Broad Hill Vineyards. Geoffrey H. Zeamer is our Winemaker and Winegrower. The Winery is located on Winter Street in Holliston, Massachusetts. The winery currently has a 17,000 liter capacity and had its first release in 2001. The winery has three vineyards where we grow our own varietals.

BROAD HILL, HIGHLAND STREET VINEYARD
Acreage: 24; Varietals Grown: Cayuga, Chancellor, Marechal Foch, and Seyval, as well as test plots of 16 additional varietals; First Plantings: 1995; Soil Type: Rainbow silt loam Micro Climate: South facing hilltop.

STONYBROOK VINEYARD
Acreage: 8; Varietals Grown: Cayuga, Chardonnay, NY 73013617, Pinot Noir, Pinot Gris; First Plantings: 2000; Soil Type: Sandy loam on glacial gravel base Micro Climate: Southeast facing hilltop and side slope.

WINTER STREET VINEYARD
Acreage: 2.9; Varietals Grown: Chelois and Chardonel: First Plantings: 2000; Soil Type: Sandy loam on glacial sand base Micro Climate: East facing hillside.

Our palette of reds is represented by four distinct types: warm and rounded, rich and dry, bright and sunny, and light and dry. This range enables you to pair a red not only with more traditional cheese and red meat, but with richer types of fish and fowl. Try the Baco Noir with Salmon or the Chelois with Halibut. From light and crisp to warm and rich, our whites offer you a broad range of flavors. On hot summer nights our crisp Chardonnay will refresh you. On a cool fall evening, try our Cayuga with figs, nuts, and cheese.

Janus, the Roman God often depicted as a double faced head, was a deity of beginnings — and is a perfect metaphor for our first vintage of champagnes. While both are dry champagnes with floral and citrus notes, they face two opposite directions. The Silver Cap (very limited production) has an exquisitely dry taste sure to appeal to the serious champagne lover, making it perfect for aperitifs. The Gold Cap (our standard) is also exquisitely dry taste, but with its delightful taste of fruit is a crowd pleaser that can take you from aperitifs through dinner and dessert.

Chancellor –
Dense, dry, ruby red and laced with pepper and cherry, underscored by aged French toasted oak. Old-world vinification techniques provide perfect tannic balance.

Chelois –
Bright and sunny this light red smells and tastes of cherries with citrus notes, and just a touch of almond in its refreshing finish.

Marechal Foch –
A light dry, red wine laced with a peppery fruity nose and a clear finish.

Baco Noir –
The taste and scent of dried currents and berries blended with soft plum notes roll across the palette in lovely harmony.

Cayuga –
With the distinctive "Highland Street" orange blossom bouquet, this wine has a creamy balance of lemon zest, and buttery notes with a subtle touch of coriander.

Chardonnay –
Diamond dry lemon-cream, rich in citrus and pale fruit, balanced with traces of oak, Broad Hill Chardonnay is vinified in the French style.

Seval Blanc –
A crisp refreshingly light wine with a lightly fruited nose, hints of melon and wood with a pleasingly smooth finish.

Diamond –
A white American with a strong nose of Concord and a pleasantly fruity finish.

Ravat 34 –
With a floral nose unique to the Highland Street vines, this fresh yet delicate wine has lovely orange and grapefruit notes, and a refreshing clean finish.

Silver Cap Extra Brut Champagne –
Bursting bubbles carry a floral bouquet and the taste of lemons balanced with warm stone and a touch of basil produce a beautifully structured dry vintage champagne.

Gold Cap Brut Champagne –
Flowers and grapefruit delicately scent this sunny dry vintage champagne. Its lemony quality is balanced by peaches and apricot notes with a subtle clean finish.

Cantina Bostonia

Cantina Bostonia
30 Germania Street, Ste A
Jamaica Plain, MA 02130
(617) 522-7595

Cantina Bostonia (Italian for Boston wine cellar) is Boston's very own winery. Owner and winemaker, Rodolfo Canale is a 1980 emigrant from Forli, Italy. Rodolfo has always been interested in good food while trying to maintain a healthy diet. He had given up drinking wine because of all of the additives but then decided to produce his own.

Quality is most important to Rodolfo, so he makes all of his wines as naturally as possible. He cleans the grapes before use and uses only natural yeasts. He had spent about seven years making smaller batches until he got the processes right. He uses Old World training with a New World twist. Taping the skills he learned as a child making wines with his father each autumn back in Italy. He markets his wines to a new breed of health conscious consumer, who do not want all of those additives and chemicals which could spoil the wine's flavor and be unhealthy. Rodolfo's wife Lovin, daughter Luana and son Robin all work at the winery, making this a true family tradition.

Our grapes come from Napa Valley and the nearby growing regions. The premium Zinfandel grapes come from Lodi. Our popular Red Table Wine is comprised mostly of moderately priced grapes such as Carignane, Alicante is added for color, and Muscat for sweetness. Barbera and Cabernet Sauvignon add depth and character. Our wines are aged in oak to add an unmistakable traditional touch. Our White Table Wine is made with Chardonnay, Chablis, Muscat and apple juice concentrate. We are the only winery that we know of that washes and dries grapes before processing. We use no sugar, sulfites or other chemicals. In Italian, the word for "vine tree" is the same as the word for "life" and the word for "heavenly" is the same as the one for "made of wine." My favorite wine for special occasions or any occasion is the Zinfandel this year (2006).

Sangiovese is the most popular wine in my home region of Italy; it is also used in the making of Chianti. My regular visits to cantinas (basements or wineries) in Romagna and Tuscany help me keep in touch with the old tradition of winemaking.

Rodolfo Canale,
Maestro del Vino

Their wines are available at local wine shops and restaurants. Cantina Bostonia is located on Germania Street in Jamaica Plain, Massachusetts. It is situated in the same colossal brick building as the Boston Beer Company, brewer of Samuel Adams beers and ales.

Cape Cod Cellars

Cape Cod Cellars
55 Linden Tree Lane
Chatham, MA 02633
(508) 945-9200
www.CapeCodCellars.com

Cape Cod Cellars a tradition of taste! In the 19th century, English and Irish seamen would rely on the assistance of French "négociants" when choosing which wines to serve at high table. Cape Cod Cellars

has brought back this tradition. We have selected wines from around the world that we feel reflect the spirit, taste and quality of Cape Cod and the islands of Nantucket and Martha's Vineyard. Through consultation with wine experts and our own research, we have selected the varietals you are sure to appreciate.

About Cape Cod Cellars:
Two families, truc tradition! What started as a family club has become a company. In 1972, we first visited Cape Cod with our cat, Whiskers, and the kids in the bucket seats of the country squire. We returned with sunburns, seashells and seaweed. Our families have been residents of either Chatham or Nantucket since the mid 1980s. As kids, well, we pretty much had most of the jobs you could imagine having. From painting on Nantucket to shucking oysters to working at a garden center to waitressing on Main Street, we had the service industries covered.

Tradition of service:
Today, our tradition of service continues through Cape Cod Cellars. We serve both the hospitality industry and consumer wine enthusiasts. Due to geographic shipping burdens placed upon many people near the Cape, we have brought the best grapes and juices to you, and negotiated a good price. Critical in the inventory selection process is the involvement and approval of the wines by some of the premier hotels on Cape Cod, Sommeliers and, we hope, you. We invite you to join in the tradition of savoring the Cape Cod life by enjoying wines from Cape Cod Cellars.

Enjoy!

Tradition of quality!

We have selected wines from around the world that we feel reflect the spirit, taste and quality of Cape Cod. We taste and select wines from various regions within the United States (e.g. Massachusetts, Virginia, New York) and abroad (e.g. Chile, New Zealand, France).

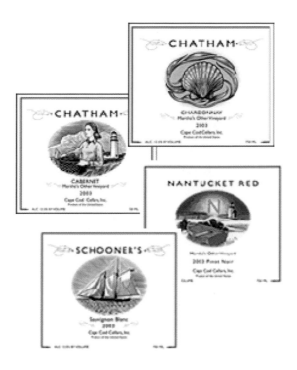

Our Wines:

Chatham Chardonnay
2002 North Coast Sonoma County Chardonnay
Our Chatham Chardonnay comes from a long line of customer favorites. Golden in color, with a fruity nose and crisp orchard flavors. Great to share with shrimp cocktail, tangy cheese and fresh apples.

Nantucket Red
2003 Merlot, Private Reserve
Bright ruby red in color with the aroma of cherry fruit and light toast. This medium bodied red shows tart berry flavors with medium tannin and heat.

Chatham Cabernet
2002 Cabernet Sauvignon, Paso Robles
Nose of well-integrated cherries and blackberries leads to intense fruit flavors in this juicy, full-bodied wine from California's warm central coast. Nicely finished with vanilla and spices from over a year in American and French Oak barrels. Enjoyed best while picnicking near one of Cape Cod's Cranberry Bogs.

Cape Cod Winery

Cape Cod Winery
681 Sandwich Road
East Falmouth, MA 02536
(508) 457-5592
www.CapeCodWinery.com

Cape Cod Winery was founded by the Lazzari family in 1994. We create premium wines for residents and visitors to enjoy with the finest seafood and gourmet cuisine available on Cape Cod. Our vineyard is

planted on a splendid site with sandy gravel soil and gentle slopes which are ideal for wine grape growing and parallel the great vineyards of southern France and northern Italy. The European vinifera wine grape varieties we have chosen are particularly suited to the special terroir of the Cape. Planted, to date, are the grape varieties Cabernet Sauvignon, Cabernet Franc, Merlot and Pinot Grigio, together with Seyval and Vidal. The extraordinary wines we produce from these fruits reflect the very special character of Cape Cod sun, soil and climate that may be savored in each sip.

Come Visit our Beautiful Vineyard and Winery in the Seaside Resort of Falmouth, Cape Cod, Massachusetts. We are open for wine tasting and sales weekends, May through December. Summer Hours are Thursday through Sunday, July 1st through August 30th 11:00 to 4:00 pm. Fall Hours are Saturday and Sunday 11:00 to 4:00 pm. Cape Cod Winery tours are Saturdays (July and August) at 2:00 pm. We have planted 6 varieties of wine grapes that grow well on Cape Cod; Cabernet Sauvignon, Cabernet Franc, Merlot, Pinot Grigio, Seyval and Vidal. We produce 2500 cases of wine annually and we won a Bronze medal for our Nobska Red wine in the International Eastern Wine Competition. Our wines are also for sale in local liquor stores. Please visit our Webpage for directions to the winery and operating hours, more information on the vineyard, descriptions of our wines and our online gift shop.

Nobska Red –
Our Cabernet blend of Cabernet Sauvignon and Cabernet Franc. This produces a full bodied red wine which we age in oak barrels for 12-18 months before bottling. It has deliciously complex flavors and a rich bouquet. This Cabernet has subtle hints of black currants, raspberries and cherries and a smooth soft finish.

Nobska White –
Our delicious Blanc de Blanc blend of Seyval and Vidal grapes has delicious tropical fruit highlights and a delicate citrus flavor and honey aroma. A perfect accompaniment to your favorite seafood dish.

Nobska Cranberry Blush –
Our luscious Seyval grape white wine with a splash of Cape Cod Cranberry Juice. Cranberries enhance the smooth and fruity character of the wine and provide a beautiful and unique rosy glow and a marvelous lingering cranberry finish.

Regatta –
Our uniquely wonderful new dessert wine; Seyval with a splash of Concord and peaches. Delicious and fruity, perfect with fresh fruit and sorbet desserts.

Merlot/Cabernet Franc –
We leave these grapes hanging on the vines as long as possible, which gives them soft and delectable red wine flavor notes of cherry and blueberry and a fabulously fruity bouquet. This blend has been delicately aged in oak barrels to give just of hint of complexity while retaining the strong deliciously fruity character of the grapes.

Pinot Grigio –
Our Pinot grapes become golden ripe giving this wine elegant gold reflections and supple character. The flavor includes delicate notes of pear, and pineapple with a fresh citrus finish. This special wine we fermented at cool temperatures to retain the enticing floral and fruit in the bouquet.

Cranberry Chardonnay –
A delicious blend of Chardonnay and a touch of cranberry makes this wine the perfect reminder of Cape Cod during the fall cranberry harvest. Excellent with turkey and chicken.

Chester Hill Winery

Chester Hill Winery
47 Lyon Hill Road
Chester, MA 01011
(413) 354-2340
www.BlueberryWine.com

Chester Hill Winery is located in Chester, Massachusetts (in the foothills of the Berkshires). Blueberries grow here in abundance and are indigenous to North America. They have been a part of the

American tradition since the pilgrims. The Native Americans associated the blueberry, or "Starberry" (just look at the star design on the bottom of one) with the Great Spirit. It was thought that starberries were sent to Earth to end a period of famine. Wild blues were eaten fresh in summer and dried or made into a paste for medicine, food, teas, juice, syrup and dye in the winter. The berries grow wild and are also cultivated within a five mile radius around the winery. Blueberry wine can be made in a variety of product styles. The wine can be made dry or sweet, still or effervescent, light or strong, and all of it is delicious.

All our wines are handcrafted in small batches to assure the highest quality. All berries are picked by hand, lightly crushed and fermented with red wine yeast. Some of the wine is made in a nouveau style to accentuate the fruitiness of the wine, which becomes our New Blue. This product is picked in July, bottled in October and is ready for the November and December holidays. It is especially wonderful with roast turkey – "An American wine for an American tradition…Thanksgiving!"

A portion of the wine is pumped into American Oak barrels where it remains for six to eight months. The oak softens the blueberry wine that is naturally high in tannins and acids. This dry wine is ready for sale the summer after the berries are picked and the winemaker considers it his Best Blue. Our port style, or Bay Blue, blueberry wine is a delight. It is a mixture of one or two year old blueberry wine and grape brandy that has been aged in oak. This wine is sweetened to bring out the flavor of the blueberries and melds well with the higher alcohol content.

We also make several white grape wines made with Vinifera and French Hybrid grapes grown in the Finger Lakes, our Mountain Laurel White and our American Riesling. Our Apple Wine is made from cider apples crushed in an Antique Cider Mill. This is a fruity, light apple wine with 10% alcohol by volume. Hard Cider was the drink of choice, or the only one affordable, in Colonial America. The only difference between Hard Cider and Apple Wine is the alcohol content. Anything greater than 8% is classified as a wine rather than a cider. We call our wine American Pie as in "As American as Apple Pie."

We are open Saturdays and Sundays from 1:00 to 5:00 pm (June through December), or by appointment. We look forward to meeting you and sharing our blueberry wine.

BLUEBERRY WINES:

New Blue –
A fruity, ruby red dinner wine with just a hint of sweetness and a lingering after taste of spices and nuts. 1.5% residual sugar. Wonderful with spicy foods, such as Mexican, Chinese, Indian and Thai, tomato sauces, grilled dishes, poultry and, of course, with turkey at Thanksgiving.

Best Blue –
A full bodied, dry, oaked blueberry wine offering hints of vanilla and toasted caramel. Ages well. 1% residual sugar. Pair with hearty cheeses such as Roquefort or Cheddar, red meats, salmon, stews and game. Enjoy with chocolates. Aged in oak.

Bay Blue –
A port-style blueberry wine for your pre-dinner and after dinner enjoyment, aged in oak and enhanced with brandy. 6% residual sweetness. Enjoy before dinner as an aperitif with Berkshire Blue cheese or Patés, or with chocolate desserts, cheese cake, or pour over vanilla ice cream. Nice in front of a fire on a cold winter's day.

MOUNTAIN LAUREL WHITES:

Seyval/Vidal Blanc –
A blend of Seyval Blanc and Vidal Blanc French Hybrid grapes. Crisp and refreshing. 1% residual sugar. A nice match with fish, seafood, white meats, goat cheeses. Bronze Medal, American Wine Society.

American Riesling –
Produced from grapes grown in the Northeast. A well-balanced wine offering flavors of sweet ripened peaches and apricots, with a rich creamy finish. 2% residual sugar. Lovely with spicy dishes, seafood, veal, chicken and cream sauces.

APPLE WINE:

American Pie –
Produced from a wide variety of apples from the "Hidden Hills" of Massachusetts to produce a wine rich in flavors. 2.5% residual sugar. It is a knockout with roast pork and other roasted meats, ham, duck, summer salads, Edam and Gouda cheeses.

Chicama Vineyards

Chicama Vineyards
191 Stoney Hill Road
West Tisbury, MA 02575
Closed September 2008

Chicama Vineyards, on the island of Martha's Vineyard, was founded by Catherine and George Mathiesen in 1971 and is operated today by three generations of the same family. It is the first bonded winery in the Commonwealth of Massachusetts. The winery produces a range of fine wines and a variety of foods including wine vinegars, mustards, chutneys and jams. Take some of our products home with you and enjoy summer memories of Martha's Vineyard - all year long!

WINERY SHOP:

All of the wines we make are available for purchase at our shop. A daily rotating selection of our wines is available for tasting. In addition to our wines, we make a variety of fine foods: wine vinegars, mustards, salad dressings, flavored oils, jams and chutneys.

During late November and all of December, our Christmas Shop is a feast for the senses: full of the sweetest of sweets and the most fragrant of spices. Taste the wines we make, and sample our mustards and sweets. Find the perfect wine for all of your holiday parties or the perfect gift for every food lover on your list.

What's new in our winery:

First on the list of jobs is bottling our Oceanus, a delicious red blend comprised of Shiraz, Merlot and Cabernet Sauvignon. We'll be bottling last fall's white wines soon after that.

What's new in our vineyards:

We are currently planning the spring 2008 planting schedule, which will involve planting vines grafted on new rootstocks in one new field and one small experimental block. The first step in both areas will be to plow and plant a soil-enriching buckwheat cover crop, which will grow over the course of this summer.

Note: Transportation to Martha's Vineyard is by ferryboat. Although foot passengers don't need a reservation, one is almost always necessary for automobiles.

RED WINES

Merlot –
This vibrant red wine is rich and flavorful without being heavy. Pair Merlot with your finest beef tenderloin or with lamb.

Oceanus –
We've blended Cabernet Sauvignon, Shiraz and Merlot to make this rich, appealing red. Enjoy it with Red Pepper Ravioli, Lamb Tagine, or Herbed Roast Chicken.

Summer Island Red –
This soft red is good for drinking right now. Take it to the beach and have with grilled Teriyaki Chicken or with your catch of the day.

WHITE WINES

Chenin Blanc –
Our off-dry Chenin Blanc is simple, straightforward and refreshing. Enjoy it as an aperitif or with spicy Thai or Chinese dishes.

Cranberry Satin –
This choice dessert wine, in glorious deep pink, will enhance pies, cobblers and pandowdies, or chocolate cake if you prefer. Try serving it over crushed ice with a twist of lemon or lime for a cranberry cooler.

Viognier –
Viognier is one of the classic Rhone varietals. This wine is rich and reminiscent of peaches, pears and apricots. Marvelous with linguini in cream sauce or a goat cheese soufflé.

Hurricane Chardonnay –
This dry white wine has a silken texture and a harmonious balance between fruit, alcohol and acidity. Serve it to friends and family with Seafood Chowder, Chicken Pot Pie or Spanish Paella.

Furnace Brook Winery

Furnace Brook Winery
508 Canaan Road
Richmond, MA 01254
(800) 833-6274
www.HillTopOrchards.com
www.FurnaceBrookWinery.com
www.JohnnyMash.com

Furnace Brook Winery is located at Hilltop Orchards, a 100 year-old farm that is a quintessential example of the open spaces that once dominated the Berkshire landscape. The Vittori family acquired the

200 acres in Richmond, MA in 1987 with a desire to ensure the preservation of the farm for generations to come. In 1998 they diversified by founding the Berkshire's first farm winery.

Now you can have award-winning Furnace Brook wines shipped to your home or office. Purchase by the bottle or by the case -- you can mix cases to customize 12 wines of your choice. Please note, there is a minimum order of 3 bottles and shipments must be in quantities of 3, 6, 12, etc. to coordinate with special FedEx shipping cartons. See why the Berkshire's First Farm Winery has become the regions' most popular. Become a Gold Wine Club Member to enjoy special savings of 15% off each club shipment

They also produce Johnny Mash, America's #1 hard cider. Made with McIntosh and Northern Spy apples. Johnny Mash has delicious oaky notes that meld magically with apple fruit on the palate. Slowly aged in American oak. Johnny Mash is a true patriot. The French Cidre' Special Reserve, is made from a blend of Golden Russet and New England apple varieties, then slowly fermented on the skins and aged in French oak barrels. Elegantly dry, remarkably complex, a real treat! Serve well chilled.

Cider pairs superbly with fish, poultry, and pork. Not only can cider be substituted for white wine in almost any recipe, but it lends an incomparable and unique flavor to dishes. Also excellent as a tenderizer or marinade. Good cheeses for cider are Smoked Gouda, Cheddar, and Jarlsberg.

The Chardonnay Special Reserve, Riesling and Muscato won medals consecutively in the 2006 and 2007 Big E Northeast Wine Competition. And in 2007 the Riesling was honored with a Gold Medal and the Cabernet Sauvignon Special Reserve and Johnny Mash were awarded for the first time with Bronze Medals.

(Kelly Colucci photos.)

Charval – A blend of Chardonnay and Seyval Blanc and is paired well with light beef, poultry and seafood, similar to the Chardonnay.

Shiraz (introduced in Jan. 2008) – Rich and full, goes nicely with hearty dishes including Indian, Mexican and other ethnic foods.

Chardonnay Special Reserve – This reserve has been lovingly aged in French oak for 18 months. Focus, finesse, balance and complexity delight in this shimmering golden award winning wine. Chardonnay is dry, and goes best with poultry or seafood, like lobster or scallops. It can even go well with a light red meat dish. Good cheeses for Chardonnay include Gruyere, Provolone, and Brie. Bronze Medal Winner Northeast Wine Competition - Big E 2007

Johannisberg Riesling – A wonderful picnic on a lazy summer afternoon - do you think of Riesling too? Semi-dry and fruity, our Northeast Varietal is best enjoyed well chilled. Riesling goes very well with oriental dishes and with seafood of all types. It is also great on its own, as a dessert wine. Good cheeses for Riesling are Hudson Valley Camembert, Sage Blue, Gruyere and Chevre Ash. Gold Medal Winner Northeast Wine Competition - Big E 2007

Sparkling Muscato – If you're looking for a wine with the perfect balance of sweetness and refreshment, you've found it. This well-rounded winner offers an "exotic aroma" that's well balanced by a crisp, refreshing finish. Our Sparkling Muscato may be enjoyed on its own before a meal and is a perfect accompaniment to spicy Thai and Italian dishes. This wine's fruity characteristics also make it the perfect match for simple desserts like fruit tarts and almond cookies. Good cheeses for Muscato are Huntsman, and Muenster. Bronze Medal Winner Northeast Wine Competition - Big E 2007

Sparkling Blanc de Blancs – Rich, smooth and delicious, a slightly fruity wine with delicate flavors. Made with a blend of Chardonnay and Seval grapes, it's a bubbly that feels luxurious and complete on the palate. 2004 Blanc de Blancs goes exceptionally well with lobster, scallops, mushrooms, light chicken, and sushi. Good cheeses for Blanc de Blancs are Brie, Chevre, Colby, and Edam.

Cabernet Sauvignon Special Reserve – If you enjoy a complex, full-bodied red wine, our Northeast Varietal Cabernet Sauvignon Special Reserve is for you. It is aged in limousine oak barrels for over 18 months and is excellent for cellaring.Cabernet goes well with beef, lamb and goose, especially when cooked with herbs. It is also a great match for Brie, Cheddar and chocolate. Bronze Medal Winner Northeast Wine Competition - Big E 2007

Merlot Special Reserve – Merlot is renowned as a dry, soft, yet full-bodied red wine. Our 2004 Merlot Special Reserve delights with its rich ruby red hue and complex character. Aged for over 18 months in limousine oak barrels. Merlot is a perfect match for beef and other medium-heavy dishes. Try some with a rich, red pasta dish, or even a heavy chicken dish. Merlot is also an excellent compliment to chocolate. Good cheeses for Merlot are Cheddar, Blue, and Colby.

Pinot Noir – Our 2004 Pinot Noir has a beautiful red hue, full of bright fruit, with a sense of harmony. Our Northeast Varietal is a red wine you can drink with food, or enjoy on its own. Pinot Noir will go well with pasta with red sauce, or lighter beef and pork dishes. Also, any local game you might have, or even goose would do well. Good cheeses for Pinot Noir are Hudson Valley Camembert, Sharp Cheddar, Parmigiano Reggiano, and Monterey Jack.

Hardwick Vineyard & Winery

Hardwick Vineyard & Winery
3305 Greenwich Road
Hardwick, MA 01037
(413) 967-7763
www.HardwickWinery.com

Hardwick Vineyard and Winery is located on a quiet country road that winds around the Quabbin Reservoir. With breathtaking floral gardens and mountain vistas surrounding you, our captivating setting adds a romantic mood for any special event or day trip.

New Englander's pride themselves with having good ol' Yankee ingenuity. So when the Samek Family purchased the 1795 Giles E. Warner farm, they restored the federal style mansion to its original splendor complete with no electricity or plumbing.

The Samek's invite you to visit their farm, vineyard, and winery. Tour the 5,000 square foot true mortise and tenon timber frame barn built with oak cut from the farm's 150 acres. Enjoy the craftsmanship of the winery's fieldstone foundation. Walk the vineyard's fields cleared in 1998 to plant the six varieties of French hybrid grapes.

Hardwick Vineyard and Winery: Where "Yankee" is our motto.

Hardwick Red Private reserve Marechal Foch –

A dry, rich bouquet of berry and plum. Full-bodied flavor. This wine will age well. Enjoy with red meats, wild game and rich sauces.

Quabbin Native –

A bright fresh fruity rose. This elegant table wine is perfect with holiday fare.

Yankee Boy White –

Slightly sweet, full bodied white wine. Rich in honey and lemon flavors. Excellent with fish, poultry or as a sipping wine.

Yankee Girl Blush –

Floral, fruity with aromas of peach and melon. This wine shows great balance of fruit and acidity. Popular accompaniment to spicy cuisine. Serve well-chilled.

Giles E. Warner –

A truly elegant wine. Delicate touches of citrus and orange peel. Dry, clean, clear, and crisp. Ideal with seafood.

Massetts Cranberry –

Delightful blend of sweet and tart. The cranberry rich flavors compliment a Thanksgiving feast served with the meal or with the dessert.

Les Trois Emme Winery & Vineyard

Les Trois Emme Winery
8 Knight Road
New Marlborough, MA 01230
(413) 528-1015 or (413) 528-2051
www.LteWinery.com

Welcome to Les Trois Emme Winery and Vineyard. We are nestled in the Berkshire Mountains in lovely New Marlborough Massachusetts. We are a family owned business that is dedicated to providing our customers with a first class wine experience with a family touch. When you visit our winery you will receive a tour and be treated to a wine tasting that pairs hors d'oeuvres with our wines that have been prepared by the family.

Try our award winning Cayuga White, an off dry white wine with a surprising apple and pear aroma and taste. It won a Silver Medal in The International Eastern Wine Competition 2007

Looking for a gift idea?
Gift cards are available for dinners, wines, and wine accessories. Or stop by our store when we are open to look at our assorted wines and wine accessories.

Candlelight Dinners!
Join us for our special event candlelight dinners in the winery as you dine on gourmet food and drink our fine wine. Multiple course meals, hors d'oeuvres, and our wines will be served in our tasting room. Seating is limited so call for a reservation to reserve a table. Visa and MasterCard are accepted to reserve dinner reservations.

Holiday Parties and Weddings: Les Trois Emme winery is a terrific place to hold a holiday or birthday party. We are also a fantastic place to hold your wedding. Have the ceremony among the vines in the vineyard and celebrate the wedding with a reception in the winery. To make arrangements please contact us.

Berkshire Red –
A dry red wine made for the Berkshire's warm days and chilly evenings.

Cayuga White –
An off dry white wine with a surprising apple and pear aroma and taste. Won a Silver Medal in the International Eastern Wine Competition 2007

Julia's Ruby Red –
A fun summer wine that cools the palate with a red berry taste.

Nick Jackson Blush –
Our blend of Cayuga white and Marechal Foch is a light blush.

Old Vine Zinfandel –
A deep, rich wine with cherry and raspberry flavors. Some would include a hint of cocoa.

Seyval Blanc –
Our dry white wine has a slight aroma of grapefruit and was aged in America Oak for 3 months.

Shiraz-Cabernet Blend –
A blend of Shiraz and Cabernet Sauvignon which displays plum and blackberry flavors.

Stingy Jack's Pumpkin Wine –
The perfect amount of pumpkin and spice blended with our Cayuga White for a truly wonderful flavor. Stingy Jack will go wonderful with Thanksgiving dinner!

Nantucket Vineyard

Nantucket Vineyard & Triple Eight Distillery
5 Bartlett Farm Road
Nantucket, MA 02584
(800) 324-5550 or (508) 228-9235
www.ciscobrewers.com/vineyard

Located in the pastoral heart of Nantucket on the way to Cisco Beach, Nantucket Vineyard was established in 1981 by Dean and Melissa Long. 2006 marked the 25th anniversary of our vineyard and we

hope you'll join us in person to celebrate our continuing success.

Part of the mission along the way has been to educate consumers about the production process involved – now islanders and visitors alike have had their consciousness expanded in regard to our fine hand-made libations. Combining old world techniques with state of the art technology Dean Long's selections include unique and delicious wines that you won't find anywhere else. No longer restricted by the islands geography and climate, Dean now finds the best grapes in the given year, and the wines are better than ever.

Triple Eight Distillery is the region's first micro-distillery. Founded by Dean and Melissa Long in 1997 and located on Nantucket Island. Triple Eight is named after its ultra pure water source, well #888, Triple Eight Distillery makes a variety of premium spirits, all of which are hand crafted in small batches using only natural ingredients. In addition to our flagship product, Triple Eight Vodka, we make Triple Eight Orange Vodka, Hurricane Rum, Gale Force Gin and Notch ("not scotch" single malt whiskey), the first release of which is due in the spring of 2005.

Our "hard stuff that's hard to get" motto is noticeably changing. Currently distributed in 12 states and growing quickly, we have recently been the beneficiary of much national media exposure (The Wall Street Journal, CNBC, Associated Press, Boston Magazine, Agenda Magazine, Elle Magazine and much more). Yet perhaps our strongest marketing force is the island of Nantucket itself and its 200,000 visitors each year. We are grateful for your continued support and look forward to your next visit to 5 and 7 Bartlett Farm Road – home of Triple Eight Distillery.

Red Wines:

2003 Sailor's Delight, Washington State –
A complex blend of Syrah and Viognier from two premier vineyards in The Columbia River Valley of Washington and Oregon reveals full luscious flavors of blackberry, prune, and jam. This wine is perfect for entertaining and enhances everyday fare from clambakes to barbeque.

2003 Merlot, Columbia River Valley, Washington State –
The grapes are from the Columbia River Appellation of Washington State. Rather dark but far from the black color seen in Merlot these days suggesting high extraction. Nose is distinctly fraise du bois with a hint of blackberry. The mouth is full bodied with fruit flavors and has a nice peppery note. Drink now or cellar for the future.

2003 Zinfandel, Lodi, California –
A famous California varietal since the 1800's, red Zinfandels are hearty and robust with flavors of black cherries and pepper. Our Zin has a vibrant nose with an aroma of ripe raspberries and nuances of oak and earthy bark.

2003 Syrah, The Dalles, Oregon –
This red grape gained its notoriety in France 's Rhone Valley . It has also become famous in South Africa and Australia , where it is called Shiraz . Syrah's are tannic and very dark in color. They abound with flavors of black currant and plums as well as black pepper and spice. The Syrah vineyards that Dean uses are located in The Dalles region of Oregon along the Columbia River Gorge. Simply put "We love it!"

White Wines:

2003 Pinot Gris Dry, Columbia River Valley Washington State –
This bottle delivers the essential character true to the Northwest style: a light-bodied white wine, crisp and vibrant, with hints of green apple, kiwi melon, and lemongrass.

2003 Chardonnay, Long Island, New York –
This is a delicious example of Long Island Chardonnay. The wine was fermented in French oak barrels and partially in stainless steel and blended prior to bottling. Wonderful flavors of citrus and pineapple and an added touch of oak yields a subtle but apparent vanilla nose. 50% barrel aged and 1000% delicious.

2003 Riesling, Westport, Massachusetts –
Riesling, a classic German grape variety, is typically dominated by aromas of honey and apricot and can be surprisingly complex in its finish. Grown in Westport, MA , outs is a very dry style wine driven by an expansive floral aroma and crisp fruit flavors. Hints of early spring earthiness compliment the light lemon and lingering berry flavors.

Sparkling Whites:

2003 Prodeano, Oregon –
With extraordinary tiny bubbles our Italian prosecco style is made with Pinot Gris and named for our vintner Dean. Prodeano has a refined sensation of drinking bubbly with light carbonation so as not to mask its rich bouquet.

Nashoba Valley Winery

Nashoba Valley Winery
100 Wattaquadoc Hill Road
Bolton, MA 01740
(978) 779-5521
www.NashobaWinery.com

Located in the heart of Massachusetts' apple country, Nashoba Valley Winery is a stunning hilltop orchard overlooking the charming town of Bolton. Always growing and ever-beautiful, we are open daily throughout the year, with the exception of The Fourth of July, Thanksgiving Day, Christmas Day and New Year's Day. Since first producing superior fruit wines in 1978, Nashoba Valley Winery has earned wide acclaim as a pioneering winery orchard and a premier destination for visitors seeking excellent wine, exquisitely prepared food, and a gorgeous country setting. The family-owned orchard, winery & restaurant, set on 52 rolling acres, boasts a state-of-the art wine-making and distillation facility, an exceptional wine and gift shop, a brewery, and a gourmet restaurant.

With over 100 national and international medals to its credit and accolades from such noteworthy publications as "Boston Magazine," "Wine Enthusiast," "Cooking Light," "Food & Wine," "Yankee Magazine" 2003 Editors Choice, and "Community Newspaper Company" 2004 Readers Choice Award, Nashoba Valley Winery is the ultimate destination for any wine connoisseur. We take the art of winemaking seriously. And with over 20 varieties of wines, a variety of hand crafted beers and distilled spirits; Nashoba Valley is dedicated to quality and is recognized as a premium producer. From its beginning until today, Nashoba Valley remains a family owned winery with our focus on quality and value at the forefront of all we do. Plan a visit to a truly unique American farm and learn why Nashoba Valley was selected as one of the ultimate destination places on the east coast.

Plan a visit to a truly unique American farm and learn why Nashoba Valley was selected as one of the ultimate destination places on the east coast.

Our commitment to you, taste our wines; elegant and dry - to complement any meal, or sweet and fruity - for apéritif or dessert. Our New England award-winning wines are delicious by themselves, and they offer some fascinating new food and wine adventures.

The process of wine making never ceases at Nashoba Valley Winery. While we continually expand our collection with each season, there are times when we may be temporarily out of certain wines. Please call our wine shop for wines that are currently available.

Sparkling Wines:
Sparkling Apple Wine

Dry Whites:
Baldwin
Chardonnay
Dry Pear
Gravenstein
Reisling
Vidal Blanc
Vignoles

Dry Reds:
Chrysleton
Dry Blueberry
Blueberry Merlot

Semi-Sweets:
Cherry
Cranberry Apple
Holiday Spiced
Cyser
Maiden's Blush
Nashoba Mead
Semi-Sweet Blueberry
Strawberry Rhubarb

Dessert:
Amora
Azule
Chancellor Port
Vidal Dessert Wine
Plum
After Dinner Peach
Raspberry

Other Nashoba Products:
New English Cider
Perry
Foggy Bog
Vodka
Cherry Brandy
Vidal Grappa
Elephant Heart
Silk
Pear Brandy
Gin "The Perfect 10"
Oak Aged Apple Brandy
Baerenfang
Northern Comfort
Elderberry Brandy
Nashoba Single Malt Whiskey

Unfamiliar with our wines? Looking for the perfect wine for dinner? You've had the Blueberry Merlot and Plum wine, but want to try the Baldwin Apple Wine? Well then, step up to the tasting bar – try before you buy! We offer a complimentary tasting where all of our guests are welcome and encouraged to enjoy samples of our delicious and unique fruit wines. Our knowledgeable staff is happy to serve you and answer all of your questions and help you make your selections. There is no fee for tasting, and reservations are not necessary.

Neponset Winery

Neponset Winery
50 Kearney Road
Needham, MA 02494
(781) 444-7780 (Winery) or
(781) 559-8061 (Business)
www.NeponsetWinery.com

Welcome to Neponset Winery, the "fruition" of a dream to start a small winery. Some people just dream; with the help and encouragement of my wife, my dream is coming true. A good friend introduced

me to winemaking more than 30 years ago. It all started with a trip to a pick-your-own berry farm. Those fresh picked currants made a pretty good wine. While I've tried my hand at making a lot of different types of wine over the years, grapes are my fruit of choice.

Neponset Winery is conveniently located in Boston's western suburbs at Exit 19B, I-95/Rt. 128. We have no vineyards. We just make fine wine from grapes grown in Massachusetts and beyond. Our Massachusetts grapes are grown in Dartmouth and Westport by one of

the best vineyardists in the northeast. A combination of the best clones for our climate, excellent "terroir," and years of experience yield grapes of superior quality with their own story.

We also source fine juice from the west coast, California, Oregon, and Washington, grown by vineyardists prized for their superior product. Some of our grapes, made into wine by west coast vineyards, sell for considerably more than ours do.

Winemaker John Comando, who lives in Needham, has been making wine at home for almost 30 years. Neponset winery is the "fruition" of a decades-long dream. We hope you'll choose to share some of that dream, visit us at the winery, and take a bottle home to enjoy.

– John Comando, Winemaker

Neponset Winery starts its third season with an exciting selection of fine wines. Our wines are made in small batches, and fermented in cold temperatures to preserve and accentuate the fruitiness of the grapes. When possible, we make our wines from locally-grown fruit. The southeastern coast of Massachusetts is garnering a reputation as an ideal place to grow fine white wine grapes that produce unique New England style wines. Stop by on the weekends to taste and purchase our wines:

2006 Unoaked Chardonnay –
Made from Massachusetts-grown grapes, fermented in stainless steel. This wine has great tropical fruit and green apple flavors with a lingering finish, and expresses all that a Massachusetts Chardonnay can be.

2006 Halloween Harvest Chardonnay –
An unusual, award-winning wine made from Massachusetts Chardonnay grapes picked on Halloween with just a touch of "noble rot." This unusual chardonnay doesn't taste like one. Flavors of Kiwi, Peaches, and Honey, with a long finish.

Pinot Gris (2006) –
Made in the Oregon style, fermented at low temperatures in stainless steel using grapes from the Suisun Valley in Northern California. Bursting with flavors of melon and honey, this is a fruity, medium bodied wine with a long finish.

2006 Rosé of Pinot Noir –
Made from Massachusetts-grown Pinot Noir pressed at harvest and fermented like our white wines. This wine is a light, low-alcohol summer sipper, a perfect accompaniment for poultry and fish.. Fruity nose with cherries and strawberries on the palate. Serve cold.

If you would like to join our email list and find out the latest news about new wine release and winery events, please visit our webpage and fill-out the opt-in form. Please note, when you receive your first email newsletter from us, you will be asked to opt-in again. This "double opt-in" is done to insure that only those that want to receive the newsletter get it.

Red Oak Winery

Red Oak Winery
325 North Main Street
Middleton, MA 01949
(978) 774-5118
www.RedOakWine.com

Red Oak Winery was founded in 2002 on the unique idea of establishing a New England winery that uses 100% Californian grapes. The winery purchases its grapes from several Californian vineyards in the Central Valley appellation. Red Oak Winery produces several white and red dry wines. Every vintage is aged in new French oak barrels that are slowly toasted over natural wood fires at specified toasting levels. Our white wines are fermented and aged in new French oak barrels, a style developed in the Bordeaux region of France. Red Oak's wine making process combines Bordeaux and California wine making styles. We do not filter any of our wines. We feel that our unfiltered wines preserve the true flavors and aromas that a fine wine should have.

Red Oak Winery's unique fermentation and long aging process captures all the flavors and aromas that a great wine has to offer. Each vintage year, Red Oak uses brand new barrels crafted from oak trees in France. The barrels are slowly toasted over natural wood fires. This process lowers tannin content and caramelizes sugars, developing aromatics and spicy flavors. Each year, we work with at least 8 different toasting levels to ensure creamy, vanillin, buttery toast flavors and well-rounded structures for our wines. Red Oak Winery works closely with our cooperage, determining the proper toasting times for our full bodied wines. This results in the rich experience of balanced oak on the nose and palate.

NEW RELEASES:

Zinfandel Reserve
Carignan
Meritage Blend
Vintner's Blend

FUTURE RELEASES:

Petit Syrah
Malbec
Classic Bordeaux Blend
Sangiovese
Super Tuscan Reserve

Red Oak's tomato pasta sauces are handmade in small kettles. Red Oak Sauces are made with Red Oak's own wines and only the best tomatoes, fresh herbs and extra virgin olive oils (a blend of oils from Italy, Spain, Greece and Tunisia) are used. The tomatoes used are the best plum tomatoes from California and Campania, Italy – the one and only San Marz and D.O.P. certified tomatoes. Just like mastering the art of making great wines with grapes from California, Frank has mastered making one of the best marinara pasta sauces on the market. Enjoy our sauces on any pasta or pizza and enjoy the experience.

Merlot Reserve – All you want in a reserve: wine - rich color, full body, concentrated flavor, firm tannins, and a long finish. Drink now or hold for 2-6 years.

Barbera Reserve – This wine is an absolute treat for the senses. The intense aroma of cherry spice, the mouth feel of soft velvet, and the finish of smooth tannins and sweet vanilla oak make this a wine that is entirely pleasing and satisfying. Even more impressive is its amazing length of flavor. Remarkable!

Cabernet Sauvignon – This true "California Cabernet" can compete with any of the famous producers in Napa. This affordable wine has everything one wants in a Cabernet: big, forward fruits of black currant, blackberries, and red licorice, a real smooth, yet bold body, and soft tannins that make this wine finish with a spicy clove, oak taste. Try this wine with red meat and other hearty fare.

Red Oak Reserve – This wine resembles perfectly matured Bordeaux. Black cherry aromas are wonderfully combined with cedar, cigar and tobacco. It has plenty of dark fruit flavors, but also toasty cedar accents that give this wine a well blended, mature feeling. The wine finishes with a lovely spicy vanilla flavor. This wine is a blend of Merlot, Cabernet Sauvignon, Zinfandel and Barbera.

Old Vine Zinfandel - The Red Zinfandel bursts of bright spicy cherry, and has a wonderful silky texture on the palette. This wine is smooth and easy to drink, and leaves a pleasant, long-lasting finish. Try this with a barbecue or with your favorite spicy dish!

Chardonnay Reserve – This richly colored wine is a real winner, distinguishable from all other Chardonnays on store shelves. The rich color of yellow is the first notable characteristic, followed by the unique and luscious flavors of pear and pineapple. The body is smooth and silky and the finish is light, intense and very pleasant.

Syrah – The brick red color indicates a wine much older and the nose is very complex and interesting. Blueberry and cherry flavors are detected but are dominated by spice aromas of clove, cinnamon and white pepper. It is a bit port-like with flavors of raisins and prunes - it has a nice acidic characteristic in the mouth.

Sauvignon Blanc/Fume Blanc Reserve – This medium-bodied wine begins with oak and cedar sweet bouquet, then tastes of honey and butterscotch, and ends with a vanilla toasty finish. It is rich and will stand up nicely to foods cooked on the grill.

Barbera – Boasts a spectacular nose of black cherry and light oak. Its medium body, fruity flavors and low tannins make this wine an easy drinking and enjoyable selection for any occasion.

Merlot – This one shines with a fine ruby red color, a chocolate covered cherry nose, and resonates with flavors of vanilla oak and a hint of coffee. This wine is smooth and silky, and has an extra long finish.

Cabernet Sauvignon Reserve – This wine's outstanding characteristics are: the dark purple color, the intense fruity nose and the grape and black currant flavors. This wine is "super smooth" - ever approachable - and finishes with a lush, velvety feel.

Vin Nouveau – The Vin Nouveau is a light, fresh wine that delights the palate with big juicy flavors of raspberries and strawberries. The iridescent pink color exemplifies its youth, and the light, fruity styles make this a wine to enjoy on any occasion. Made the same way as the well-known Beaujolais Nouveaus from France.

Running Brook Vineyards & Winery, Inc.

Running Brook Vineyards & Winery, Inc.
335 Old Fall River Road
North Dartmouth, MA 02747
(508) 985-1998
www.RunningBrookWine.com

Welcome to Running Brook Vineyards & Winery, Inc. We are a premier winery located in North Dartmouth Massachusetts. Our vineyards are located in Westport and Dartmouth Massachusetts. At Running Brook, we produce fine still and sparkling wines from our own grapes. We currently have Chardonnay, Merlot, Cabernet Franc, Pinot Noir, Pinot Gris, and Vidal Blanc vines in production.

Running Brook Vineyards and Winery, Inc. was founded in 1998 by Pedro Teixeira and Manuel Morais out of a vision to produce top quality wines that will make New Englanders proud and satisfy their palates.

Dr. Pedro Teixeira (Owner) graduated from The Ohio State University College of Dentistry in 1987. Having spent most of his childhood in the Azores, Portugal and later California he caught the grape bug. This condition exacerbated when he moved to Rhode Island and met his patient, now partner, Manuel Morais. They visited many vineyards and wineries and decided to grow Vitis Vinifera grapes and produce premium wines in Southeastern New England.

Mr. Manuel Morais (Owner and Vineyard Manager) was born and raised in Azores, Portugal. One of his fondest memories as a child was going with his father to the vineyard. By the age of thirteen he began grafting for his father and soon the older viticulturists in town began to notice his talent for grafting. Two or three years later, everyone wanted Manuel to graft for them. Before long, he was grafting for the whole town. Grafting became quite natural for Mr. Morais. In 1975, Mr. Morais was one of the first in New England to start a vineyard. Recently he invented an idea that may revolutionize the vineyard industry in cool viticultural regions called "tall grafts." Today, Running Brook has established vinifera vineyards in both Westport and Dartmouth Massachusetts.

2004 Chardonnay – This cool climate New England style Chardonnay is acid driven and aged for 2 years in old French oak giving it a clean, crisp fruity taste balanced with full bodied light oak flavor and 100% malolactic fermentation.

2002 White Merlot – This fine wine is made in the same method as a White Zinfandel or a White Burgundy. The fruit is pressed with light skin contact giving it its light red color. The wine is fermented and aged for 2 years in stainless steel. Our dry white merlot is acid driven and reminiscent of a French Rosé.

2002 Cabernet Franc – Cabernet Franc, one of the great wines of French varietals, lends itself well to growing in our cool climate. Our wine with its European reminiscent style makes it compatible with a wide variety of foods. This acid driven wine, combined with balancing light tannins and ripe fruity flavors tantalizes both the nose and palate.

2001 Celebration Sparkling Wine – This sparkling wine was established in the year of the millennium with the goal of producing premium wine. Our soils and cool New England climate are perfectly suited to produce sparkling wine being most similar to Northern France and other great wine producing regions. Our wines are made in the traditional method or "Methode Champenoise" restricted by the Appellation of d'Origine Controlee and represent world class quality and excellence. Our intention is to give you the best wine experience and we hope you will join in our Celebration.

2003 Cabernet Franc Merlot – Two of the great French varietals, both lend themselves well to growing in our cool climate. Our unique blend with its European reminiscent style, make it compatible with a wide variety of foods. This lightly acid driven wine, combined with balancing light tannins and fruity richness tantalizes the nose while leaving as delectable impression on the palate. This wine is a blended of 60% Cabernet Franc and 40% Merlot.

2005 Frost Wine – A late harvest dessert wine made from Vidal grapes and comprised of 10% alcohol, 10% sugar and 28% brix at harvest. Produced from ripe grapes that have been left on the vine and then frozen; the grapes are pressed in such a way that the frozen water remains in the press leaving juice that is highly concentrated in sweetness and acidity.

2006 Auslesen – Auslese [OWS-lay-zuh] is the German word for "selection." It is used in the wine trade to describe specially selected, perfectly ripened bunches of grapes that are hand-picked and then pressed separately from other grapes.

2005 Pinot Gris – Our 2005 Pinot Gris is a crisp, full bodied wine with citrus overtones and a wonderful, clean finish. We believe this is one of the best Pinot Gris available anywhere!

2005 Vidal Blanc – New this year for Running Brook, the 2005 Vidal Blanc starts with a crisp fruit taste which evolves into a semi-dry, dynamic finish. It is a surprisingly versatile white wine.

2004 Petit Verdot – One of the great French varietals, lends itself well to growing in our cool climates. Our wine with its European reminiscent style makes it compatible with a wide variety of foods. This acid driven wine, combined with balancing light tannins and ripe fruity flavors tantalizes both the nose and palate.

Russell Orchards Farm & Winery

Russell Orchards Farm & Winery
143 Argilla Road
Ipswich, MA 01938
(978) 356-5366
www.RussellOrchardsMA.com/winery.php

The Russell Orchards property has a long history as a working farm. As the third family that has owned the farm since its creation in 1920, we, the Russell family, are honored to continue its long tradition. The winery began with the acquisition of a farm winery license in 1988. We introduced traditional New England hard ciders in three flavors: Dry, Sweet, and Slightly Sweet. As we have expanded upon our fruit production at the Orchard, we have added many new fruit wines. Our goal is to

produce traditional wines most commonly found on farms throughout the United States and Europe over the past 300 years. As our listing of wines indicates, fruit wines are excellent for drinking, sipping, and sharing at meals. There is a wide variety of flavor, sweetness, and unique characteristics not found in grape wines. Among our selection of fruit wines we have learned that there is a variety for every palate. Just try them - you will enjoy them! Wine tastings are always available in our farm store.

All of our unique fruit wines and hard ciders are made on the premises with our own fruit. The only exceptions are the Blueberry and Dry Blueberry varieties, which use Wild Maine Blueberries. Our hard ciders are made from our own Baldwin apples and the Perry is made from our own Bosc pears. They can be enjoyed for sipping, cooking, and are an excellent accompaniment to any meal. The serving suggestions offered below have been compiled from years of our own tasting and from the comments of the many folks who have tried our wines at the wine counter. Please come in to the store and taste for yourself.

In addition to the many varieties of berries, peaches, pears, cherries, and, of course, apples, we offer "no-spray" vegetables, herbs and tomatoes from our greenhouse and garden! If we don't grow a particular vegetable, we always try to buy locally grown veggies from our farmer friends, organic whenever possible. The farm is comprised of 120 acres of fields, gardens, orchards, and barns. The farm is in a continual state of improvement and growth. Scores of new trees are grafted and transplanted every year, as we strive to reach the enormous potential for productivity that the land offers. Although owned by the Russell Family, the Essex County Greenbelt Association holds an agricultural restriction on Russell Orchards and consequently it will never be developed. We grow most of what we sell in the store and we buy local produce whenever possible. It is important to us to support other small local businesses whenever we can. See our Webpage to find out what fruits and vegetables are in season. Check back often to see Pick-Your-Own availability. All containers are provided and children are welcome. Remember to always call ahead for pick your own hours and availability. Fruit picked ripe from the farm is a whole different experience!

(Photo by Miranda Russell)

Fruit Wines (11% Alcohol):

Apple-Blueberry – A delicate combination of our Baldwin Apple and Wild Blueberry with a refreshing, light flavor. Great with poultry, sipping.

Baldwin Apple – A dry white wine, similar to a crisp chardonnay. Pork, chicken, or pasta.

Black Currant – A distinctive, fruity nose and strong, sweet currant flavor. Dessert.

Blackberry – Mellow, rounded, and gently flavored. Lamb or turkey.

Blueberry – Made from wild Maine blueberries. A wonderful Merlot type red wine that is superb with any meat. Roast beef, leg of lamb.

Cherry – Light and dry with a hint of almond. Fish, pork, cheese.

Dry Blueberry – Similar to the Blueberry, except this wine is aged in French oak. Bold like a Cabernet with a subtle berry flavor. Red meat.

Dandelion – Unique flavor has the essence of sherry wine. With any meal, as a dessert wine, or by itself.

Elderberry – Dry robust wine with a smooth lingering berry flavor. Venison, red meat.

Jostaberry – The berry is a cross between the gooseberry and the black currant. This wine has a mellow, fruity taste. Venison, roast beef, duck.

Peach – This semi-dry wine boasts a light peach flavor. Pork, chicken, or pasta.

Raspberry-Peach – This fresh wine is a combination of our excellent peach wine and the full-bodied raspberry. Appeals to Zinfandel drinkers. Excellent after dinner or with any meal.

Red Currant – Tart with a clean, strong currant taste. Poultry; a favorite at holiday meals.

Rhubarb – A sweet dessert wine made from an old farm recipe. Made with fresh-picked rhubarb from our garden. Fish, pork, and poultry; sipping.

Strawberry-Rhubarb – This complex yet delicate picnic wine is delicious. Fish, or any white meat.

Hard Ciders and Perry (7-8% Alcohol):

Dry – A traditional dry New England cider. Similar to our Baldwin Apple wine, but with less alcohol. Chicken, fish.

Slightly Sweet – Very popular with an easy taste. Similar to a good European cider. Sipping or cooking.

Cider/Perry – A mellow blend of apples and pears. Taste is similar to our Slightly Sweet Cider. Chicken, fish, or pork.

Sparkling – Award winning sparkling dry wine made in the traditional Methode Champenoise. (8% alcohol.) Excellent with meals or any festive occasion.

Truro Vineyards

Truro Vineyards
PO Box 834, Route 6A
North Truro, MA 02652
(508) 487-6200
www.TruroVineyardsofCapeCod.com

Truro Vineyards has been in operation since 1992. Cape Cod's beautiful summer weather makes for great vacations – and great wine! We pioneered the art of maritime grape growing on the Cape, and our

vinifera vineyard produces wine with intense flavor and lush varietal character. We open our doors each season to wine lovers from around the world who visit the tasting room and gift shop in our carefully restored 1830's farmhouse.

The vineyard founders, Kathy Gregrow and Judy Wimer, dreamed of growing grapes on Cape Cod. They believed that the Cape could potentially be a good area for grape cultivation. In the early 1990's, they spotted the property for sale and purchased what would become Truro Vineyards. Armed with degrees in plant science and previous horticultural experiences, Kathy and Judy began converting the farm into a commercial vineyard. Besides planting the vineyard, they renovated the house and barn to accommodate the tasting room and winery production area. After fourteen years, their hard work has paid off with the fulfillment of their very own American dream.

Kathy and Judy worked hard for years to create fine wines and a beautiful Cape Cod experience for visitors. Recently, they sold the winery and vineyard to the Roberts family, and have been working closely with them to ensure a smooth transition. "Kathy and Judy have created a wonderful wine country experience here in North Truro," says new owner Dave Roberts. "We plan to simply enhance what they have already done so well."

During the summer, wine tastings are held outdoors under our tasting tent near the vineyard. Sit down and relax as we explain the nuances of wine and lead you through our selection of nine wines. In season, guided tours of the vineyard and winery are offered as well. Tours are at 1pm and 3pm from May to October.

We invite you to stop by and experience our fine wines, stroll through our vineyards and picnic on our beautiful grounds. Browse through our newly expanded gift shop and discover an interesting assortment of wine accessories, exclusive lines by local artists and fine food products.

- Dave Roberts, Kathy Roberts, David Roberts Jr.,Kristen Roberts, Amy Roberts and Stephanie Roberts Hartung

Some of our wines:

2005 Truro Vineyards Triumph –
Grapes: Cabernet Sauvignon-Merlot-Cabernet Franc blend; Barrel Aging 18 months in American oak. Awards: 2006 Tasters Guild Silver Medal, 2005 International Eastern Wine Competition Bronze Medal; Tasting Notes: Bordeaux-style blend with classic black fruit concentration: black cherry, blackberry, and a hint of dark roasted coffee in the finish. Good tannic structure, plenty of inviting oak, smooth and elegant texture. Alcohol 12.5%

2005 Truro Vineyards Maritime Red –
Grapes: Merlot-Zinfandel-Cabernet Franc blend. Fermentation Extended maceration in open vats followed by fermentation in open vats. Barrel Aging 18 months in American oak. Awards: 2006 Tasters Guild Silver Medal; Tasting Notes: Soft, pleasing fruity aromas a little like Gamay. Rich ripe plum flavors, bright raspberry and blackberry. Good tannic structure, lots of spicy herbal flavors in the finish. Superb with hearty grilled meats, game, or flavorful pasta dishes. Alcohol 12.5%

2005 Truro Vineyards Cabernet Franc –
Grapes: 100% estate-grown Cabernet Franc. Appellation Southeastern New England. Fermentation Handpicked, crushed and fermented in open vats in the traditional Loire style. Prolonged skin contact for optimal color, flavor and tannin extraction. Barrel Aging 20 months in American oak. Awards: 2006 Tasters Guild Silver Medal, 2005 International Eastern Wine Competition Silver Medal; Tasting Notes: Medium-bodied, dry red wine with woodsy herbal character, black cherry, raspberry, and smooth toasted oak. Serve with grilled meats and flavorful cheeses. Alcohol 12.5%

2005 Truro Vineyards Chardonnay –
Grapes: 100% Chardonnay. Fermentation Barrel fermented in small American oak barrels with frequent battonage (stirring) by hand and extended aging on the lees. Awards: 2005 Tasters Guild Bronze Medal, 2004 Tasters Guild Silver Medal; Tasting Notes: Toasty oak aromas with layers of ripe apple and vanilla. Finish is long, warm and slightly citrusy. Serve lightly chilled with broiled seafood, lobster, roasted poultry, and pastas with cream sauce. Alcohol 12%

NV Truro Vineyards Sauvignon Blanc –
Grapes: 100% Sauvignon Blanc. Fermentation Cold fermented in stainless steel. Awards: 2006 Tasters Guild Bronze Medal; Tasting Notes: Bright golden color, clear and radiant. Aromas of white flowers, pear, peach and honeydew melon. Nice tropical zip and zing typical of Sauvignon Blanc. Perfect served well chilled with oysters, clams, mussels, grilled fish and spicy cuisine. Alcohol 13.5%

NV Truro Vineyards Vignoles –
Grapes: 100% Vignoles. Awards: 2006 Tasters Guild Gold Medal, 2005 Tasters Guild Gold Medal; Tasting Notes: Lots of tropical fruit aromas like pineapple, guava, even a little coconut. A nice layer of crisp citrus gives wine good lift and nice balance with the rich fruit. The Vignoles grape produces some of the most interesting semi-dry and dessert wines in North America. This is a great match with spicy, exotic, hard-to-match Asian cuisines, but it also works beautifully as a light dessert wine with a fresh berry tart or crème brulée. Alcohol 11.5%, Residual Sugar 3%

NV Truro Vineyards Cape Blush –
Grapes: Cayuga-Cabernet Franc blend. Fermentation Cold fermented in stainless steel utilizing a strain of Riesling yeast. Tasting Notes: Charming salmon color, inviting aromas of strawberry, cherry, and peach. Nicely balanced with pleasing semi-sweetness and nice citrus zing. Perfect for summer sipping, great at any beach picnic, barbecue, or casual event. Serve well chilled with mild cheeses, hors d'oeuvres, poultry and pork. Alcohol 11%, Residual Sugar 2%

231

Turtle Creek Winery

Turtle Creek Winery
PO Box 691
Lincoln, MA 01773*
(781) 259-9976
www.TurtleCreekWine.com

TURTLE CREEK
Lincoln, Massachusetts

Turtle Creek Winery is a small winery located in the shadow of Boston. Our plantings include Chardonnay, Cabernet Franc, Pinot Noir, and Riesling. We also purchase fruit from California and the Finger Lakes.

Some years ago, French traditionalists coined the phrase *vin de garage* as a pejorative term to describe the burgeoning phenomenon of small scale wineries whose wines did not represent known terroirs and who had no previously established brand recognition. A few of these wines quickly garnered outstanding reviews. In France these wineries include Chateau le Pin in Pomerol, which produced its first vintage in 1979, and Claude Dugat in Cotes de Nuits. In Italy, Tenuta di Trinoro. In California are Screaming Eagle, Marcassin and Colgin Cellars. All these garagistes have in common a small scale (usually less than 2000 cases per year), extraordinary quality and a passion for the craft of viticulture and winemaking.

At Turtle Creek we welcome this appellation. Small scale wineries, while accounting for a negligible share of market for wine production, are nevertheless at the leading edge of innovation. At larger volumes of production, it is simply not possible to devote the attention to detail which is feasible at a smaller scale. In most wineries and viticulture, decisions are always a tug-of-war between quality and economics. At Turtle Creek quality is an uncompromising criterion. Clonal selection, yield per vine, fruit thinning, ripening criteria, hand picking and sorting, batch size, new French oak, gentle handling of must and wine

with peristaltic and progressive cavity pumps—all are examples of stark differences between the way we go about our work and that of the typical medium to larger winery; all these choices speak to our passion for the craft.

*There is no tasting room at the winery and visits are limited to occasional private tastings and tours. We announce new releases by email. If you would like to receive announcements, please send us your email address.

Mirabile dictu! In vino narration,
(In wine is the story, marvelous in the telling).

Kip Kumler, Owner, Winemaker, Garagiste

232

TURTLE CREEK NEWS - July 2007
There is good news and there is bad news. First, the bad news: we are sold out of all wines at the winery. This is the first time, in our brief history, that we have not had any wines on hand at the winery for sale. This is not good because it is always disappointing to try to find wines you have had or heard about and not be able to purchase them - people find other wines of interest and memories fade... The fact that we do not have wines for sale here does not mean none are available at the outlets listed on our website.

The good news is that we have increased our production by 100% for the 2006 vintage which brings us just under 1000 cases where we expect to stay forever. In addition, the 2006 vintage brings small quantities of our own grapes, including Cabernet Franc, Riesling and Chardonnay with a vineyard - designated label: "Conservation Hill" from our main vineyard in Lincoln.

RESEARCH NEWS –
We are publishing our research online with full disclosure and in the spirit of sharing it with anyone who has an interest; indeed, our hope is that our experience can contribute to new ideas from others and that, in the end, everyone gains some benefit and that we all make better wine. In 2004 we began an ambitious effort to study and implement various means of protecting Vitis Vinifera vines in a New England winter.

OUR WINES:

Turtle Creek Winery strives to produce excellent, hand-crafted wines combining traditional techniques with modern technology to preserve the integrity of the grape. We restrict vineyard yield, hand sort, and vinify our wines in the most gentle way. Please check our webpage for more information on our wines.

New Releases:
Two 2006 Chardonnays and two 2006 Rieslings, one each from our own Lincoln grapes.

Westport Rivers Vineyard & Winery

Westport Rivers Vineyard & Winery
417 Hixbridge Road
Westport, MA 02790
(508) 636-3423 ext. 2 or (800) 993-9695
www.WestportRivers.com

Westport Rivers is a family owned vineyard and winery producing estate grown wines from New England's largest vineyard. Our wines include traditional method sparkling wine, Chardonnay, Rosé of  Pinot Noir, Riesling and other Alsatian varietals. We are best known for sparkling wines which rival any from around the globe. As Madeleine Kamman (Chef, Educator and Award-Winning Cookbook Author) has noted, "They can't do this in California; many in France are not this good." In addition, we make a variety of exciting table wines. In particular, our chardonnay is stylish with wonderful acidity and lots of fruit. The New York Times notes that our chardonnay is "virtually flawless."

Westport Rivers began in 1982 when Bob & Carol Russell bought an old dairy farm in Westport, Massachusetts. Several years later, the vines arrived as did their oldest son, Rob. Rob and his crew planted the first vines in 1986 and our vineyard has grown into the largest vineyard in New England (and it is all vinifera). Bill Russell, Bob & Carol's second son, joined the team in 1989 to begin making wine. The winery opened to the public during the summer of 1991.

Many wine lovers are discovering that cool climates create the most dramatic sparkling, white and rosé wines in the world. The classic cool climate style of a natural, crisp, refreshing balance between fruit and acidity is the hallmark of all of Westport Rivers' wines. We don't get in the way and overtly stylize our wines with gobs of oak or sweetness. We aim to allow the terroir of the vintage shine through; we want the wine to taste like the grapes from which it was created. Most Westport Rivers wines are fermented in stainless steel, which keeps the focus on the grapes and the vintage. Our wines are celebrated for refreshing the palate and pair well with many foods. Cheers!

Sparkling Wine – Our sparkling wines are amongst the finest made in the United States

2002 Brut Cuvée RJR – 63% Estate Grown Pinot Noir & 37% Estate Grown Chardonnay
This is the wine that put Westport Rivers on the map. Each vintage is extraordinary for its' own rights. The 2002 has lovely, frothy mousse with aromas of ripe apples, pear, toast and cream. A deliciously soft, creamy finish begs for just one more sip. A wine to entice you from start to finish.

2000 Blanc de Noirs – 87% Estate Pinot Noir, 13% Estate Pinot Meunier
Lovely salmon colored wine with simply gorgeous flavors of berries and cream. Soft supple fruitiness gives way to a focused, clean finish.

1999 Blanc de Blancs – 100% Estate Chardonnay Conceived and born into existence as the perfect wine for oysters. Ultra Brut clean, crisp, apples and toast. Balanced with feather-like delicateness.

2001 Imperial Sec – 88% Estate Grown Riesling, 12% Estate grown Rkatsiteli
Typical brassy color with very, very small bubbles. Delicious and fresh nose, showing wonderful floral character with a touch of citrus. On the palate, crisp fruit with a hint of sweetness.

1992 Cuvée Maximilian – 78% Estate Grown Pinot Noir with 22% Estate Grown Chardonnay
An incredible "RD" style with 14 years "en triage." Huge, smooth, complex; this wine deserves to be called Max. Comes in its own custom box.

Other Wines

2006 Westport Rivers Riesling Release –
The last Westport Rivers Riesling was the 2002 vintage. Now, we are pleased to release this wonderful wine. Riesling, embrace the exotic flavors of summertime. Westport Rivers 2006 Riesling has beautiful aromas of pineapple, kiwi and orange peel with a generous palate of ripe fruit and crisp acidity. Finishes with a lingering citrus kick.

2006 Rosé of Pinot Noir – 100% Estate Grown Pinot Noir
Attractive bright rose color, the wine has a fascinating, complex bouquet with berries, rose petal and a touch of cotton candy. The palate is generous - round and soft yet brisk and firm with wonderfully balanced acidity and richness. The wine finishes with a lingering fruitiness. Our most versatile food wine - pairs well with many dishes from vegetarian to beef and spicy, smoky flavors or exotic spices in Indian and Thai food.

2006 Pineau de Pinot – Estate Grown Pinot Noir juice blended with Estate Grown Eau de Vie
Delicious. Fruity. Like no aperetif/dessert wine you've likely ever had. We are able to capture the pure essence of the vintage by blending some of our specially distilled estate grown eau de vie with pinot noir juice. The result is sure to blow you away.

2005 Rkatsiteli –
The great wine grape of Russia, Rkatsiteli, is the sixth most planted white grape of the world yet nearly unheard of in the United States. Wonderful acidity, a pleasant spicy, floral character and a hint of sweetness make this wine simply delicious.

Candia Vineyards

Candia Vineyards
702 High Street*
Candia, NH 03034-2040
(603) 867-9751
www.CandiaVineyards.com

CANDIA VINEYARDS

Candia Vineyards is a boutique vineyard that specializes in fine table wines from grapes. Our products, processes, and labels are meant to convey our dedication to hard work, quality, history, and romance. With traditionally correct food pairings, our wines transform a good meal into a memorable one. Social occasions are enhanced by the inclusion of a favorite Candia Vineyards wine, and many a romantic interlude has been heightened by our wine.

Romance begins with New Hampshire's first Frontenac, Lacrosse, Noiret, LaCrescent, Marquette, and Diamond varietals. Our selections have been hand-picked to thrive in the robust New Hampshire climate. This matching of grapes to our local growing conditions, combined with our carefully developed processes for hand-crafting our wines, has brought Candia Vineyards numerous medals in many national and international competitions.

Our town is steeped in folklore, in which it has been told that a party of hunters in the mid-1700's felled a fine deer, which they proclaimed to be charming fare. The town was then named Charmingfare. The subsequent naming of "Candia" is for the Mediterranean town of Candia on the Isle of Crete, where a New Hampshire governor spent some time "on reserve". Legend has it that he thought it was such a beautiful place that he renamed our town Candia when he returned. Our Vault Reserve wines forever immortalize this legend with label artwork depicting historic characters and our wine vault! Look for our Vault Reserve selections as we release our specialty wines.

Candia Vineyards is sited on some of the earliest farmed land in New Hampshire. This rich tradition of farming is something that we are very proud of, and we feel is particularly important here in southern New Hampshire, where development pressures are so intense. This heritage merits preservation, and we proudly do our part to show that hard work and careful attention to quality are worthwhile pursuits.

We use the highest quality grapes, premier oak, and highly refined methods – no matter what the cost. Our goal is the best quality grapes and wine that captures the lure of rural New Hampshire and the romance of enjoying wines with your special guests. We're one of the smallest operations in the US, but we are big on business ethics, and this is the guiding force that inspires us every day. We were awarded *Best of NH 2008 by New Hampshire Magazine, earning dozens of medals in 2008, and the most awarded small winery at the Eastern States Exposition.* *Tours by appointment, please call (603) 867-9751 or email: Bob@CandiaVineyards.com

Noiret
A classic dry red wine with unusually intense overtones of pepper. With its wonderful aromas, our Noiret is the most consistently awarded of this varietal in the world! Medals: Eastern States 2007 & 2008, Indianapolis International 2007, Atlantic Seaboard 2007, Florida State Fair 2008, Finger Lakes International 2008, International Eastern 2008

Frontenac
Bred at the University of Minnesota from Landot Noir, it is one of the most significant grapes developed in the 1990's. Our award winning Frontenac has unusually intense fruit overtones that belie its classic dryness.

LaCrescent
Stunning. A sweeter wine with wonderful aromas that you'll never forget. One of NH's rarest wines, we are proud to be the first to offer this fine varietal. A medal winner at the Finger Lakes International wine competition.

Diamond
Also known as Moore's Diamond, it was developed by Jacob Moore of Brighton, New York, in 1885. The wine was popular in NY many years ago, and was known as the first quality dry wine produced from American grapes. This all but forgotten grape was brought back into production at Candia Vineyards where it delights the unsuspecting with an intense aroma. Candia Vineyards makes this in a fruity semi-sweet style which complements your favorite spicy Asian cuisine.
2005 Indianapolis International Wine Competition Silver Medal; 2006 International Eastern Wine Competition Silver Medal; 2006 Indianapolis International Wine Competition Bronze, International Eastern 2007, Finger Lakes International 2008.

LaCrosse
A dry white wine with intense flavors, LaCrosse is a big hit on the lakes or by the seaside! Enjoy it with that special lobster, oyster or fish dinner.

Good King Robert's Red & Classic Cab
Two of our rich, bold reds. Invite Good King Robert to an intimate steak dinner with someone special, or take a Classic Cab to join Friends for a hearty, and heart-warming, stew. Both of these multiple award winners can be enjoyed without the meal, but good company is definitely recommended.

Farnum Hill Ciders

Farnum Hill Ciders
98 Poverty Lane
Lebanon, NH 03766
(603) 448-1511
www.FarnumHillCiders.com

Farnum Hill Cider fulfills the true meaning of the word "cider" -- an alcoholic beverage fermented from apples, exactly as a wine is fermented from grapes. Our own ciders, at 6.5-7.5% alcohol, tend toward the dry, sharp, fruity and bountifully aromatic. We intend them to gladden the moment and to freshen the flavors of companionable foods. We are proud of Farnum Hill Ciders, and we are authoritatively told that, for now at least, they are the best-made ciders in America.

We hope and expect that more Eastern apple-growers will learn the craft and horticulture of cider making, and that distinctive American orchard-based ciders, now too rare, will return to their pre-Prohibition glory and variety. Johnny Appleseed planted the frontier for cider, after all -- "Mom and apple pie" came later, blotting out certain enjoyable truths from the national memory. But now cider -- real cider -- is back.

Traditional Ciders from True Cider Apples

Farnum Hill Ciders are dry and complex, wine-like but, at 6.5-8.5%, less alcoholic than grape wines. (Most dry wines contain between 11% and 15% alcohol.) On Farnum Hill we grow true cider apples of English, French, and American origin. Peculiar-tasting when fresh, cider apples produce gorgeous aromas, flavors and sensations after pressing, fermenting, and blending by the respectful cidermaker. The English and European varieties that flourish here attain highly concentrated flavors in this extreme New Hampshire climate.

What is a Cider Apple?

Just as serious winemaking requires vintage grapes, serious cidermaking requires certain apples never found in the family fruit bowl. Cider apples are barely beginning a return to U.S. orchards, but back in the Old World, many varieties are grown for both specialty and mass market ciders.

Vintage apples offer :
High tannins, for bitterness, astringency, and "body."
High sugars, for alcohol production.
Sufficient acid for full flavor and balance.
Pleasing apple taste and aroma.

English-speaking cider makers describe cider apples as bittersharp, bittersweet, sharp, or sweet,* ranked as "full, medium, or mild," according to the levels and combinations of acids, tannins, and sugars in their juice. All contain a lot of sugars, often masked by acidity or bitterness. Biting into most of them is a bad experience.

*Sharp and bittersharp varieties contain more than 0.45% malic acid, while sweet and bittersweet varieties normally fall below this level. Sweet and sharp varieties contain less than 0.18% tannin; bittersweet and bittersharp varieties, more than 0.18% tannin. All offer high sugars, or should.

From different cider apples our ciders draw their myriad aromatic charms. For centuries, blending has been the name of the game, though exceptional apples such as Kingston Black are famed for giving excellent "single-variety" cider.

Hundreds of cider apple varieties have been found, developed, propagated, described, discussed, promoted, lost and sometimes found again. In our orchards we test more varieties all the time, seeking those that grow well on our hill in our weathers. So often, the same fruit grows gorgeously in one place and boringly in another, or vice-versa. Under apple varieties are listed, by category, some of the cider varieties growing here. We haven't tried to evoke the mysterious aromatic qualities of each -- words fail.

On Farnum Hill, overlooking the Connecticut River in New Hampshire, we grow true cider apples of English, French, and American origin. Peculiar-tasting when fresh cider apples produce gorgeous aromas, flavors and sensations after pressing, fermenting, and blending by the respectful cidermaker.

243

Flag Hill Winery & Distillery

Flag Hill Winery & Distillery
297 North River Road, Route 155
Lee, NH 03861
(603) 659-2949
www.FlagHill.com

Flag Hill Winery & Distillery was established in 1990. This scenic spot in Lee, New Hampshire has been a working farm since the 1700s. In 1990, it became Flag Hill Farm & Vineyard with the planting of the first acre of grapes. An aggressive planting schedule has continued since that date. The very first harvest occurred in 1994 with all the fruit being sold to the New Hampshire Winery in Henniker, NH. The 1995 harvest was processed, stored, and vinted by Flag Hill.

In the spring of 1996, Flag Hill Winery was established with a production of 500 cases consisting of four types of wine, and the doors to the winery were opened. In addition to the winery Flag Hill is also a working distillery, with its first product, General John Stark Vodka, hitting the market in December of 2004. With this foray into the arena of spirits, Flag Hill continues its path of growing and embracing new ventures. We also make Sugar Maple Liqueur. The sweet taste of New Hampshire Maple Syrup blended with the very best of General John Stark Vodka. A sweet sensation with a kick!

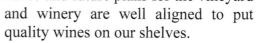

Flag Hill's vineyard stretches over 20+ acres of land on slightly sloping terrain. We continue to plant the best-suited grapes for our erratic New England climate. Not all grapes can survive the drastic dips of temperature that winter brings. Our vineyard produces 6 varieties of grapes including North American, such as Niagara, French Hybrid such as Marechal Foch and Vignoles, and American Hybrid such as Cayuga. The owner, winemaker, and vineyard manager work closely together as a team to ensure performance and future plans for the vineyard and winery are well aligned to put quality wines on our shelves.

Flag Hill has grown from a family operated vineyard to an established winery in the picturesque seacoast region of NH. Make Flag Hill a destination to learn how our vodka is made first hand, taste from a variety of NH made wines, stroll through the vineyard, picnic on the grounds, or browse through our gift shop.

244

Apple Cranberry -
Sweet New Hampshire apples and tart Massachusetts cranberries unite in a crisp fruit wine.

Plum -
A semi-sweet wine with the flavor of freshly picked plums.

Red Raspberry -
A sweet berry red fruit wine with deep notes of raspberry.

Seyval Blanc -
A semi-dry white wine that features citrus, peach and a touch of honeysuckle with a fresh, clean finish.

Vignoles -
A crisp semi-sweet white wine, with notes of melon and pear.

Cayuga White -
A bright semi-sweet white, layered with citrus and exotic fruit with a well-balanced acidity that lingers nicely.

Niagara Reserve -
Native American white grapes, aged in American oak barrels for six months.

Niagara -
A white Native American grape, foxy on the nose, mixed with notes of honey and green apple on the palate. Classic style and elegance.

Marechal Foch -
Medium bodied red wine with deep, dark color of the French Hybrid grape.

Chancellor -
A light semi-sweet red wine with similar characteristics to a Beaujolais style wine.

Heritage Red -
A smooth, mellow and sweet red dessert wine blended with pure NH maple syrup. Fragrant with a black cherry/nutty aroma.

Heritage White -
A sweet white dessert wine ripe with the aroma of native grapes, blended with pure NH maple syrup. Serve warm or cold.

North River Port -
New Hampshire's first classic port. Aged in oak six years, this special port has qualities of black licorice, clove and layered almond, and balanced oak ending with a perfect amount of heat.

Blueberry Moon –
Wild Maine blueberries presented as an after dinner beverage. An enticing taste on its own, this savory wine made in a port styling is the fine compliment to the end of any great meal.

Jewell Towne Vineyards

Jewell Towne Vineyards
65 Jewell Street
South Hampton, NH 03827
(Entrance at 183 Whitehall Rd.)
(603) 394-0600
www.JewellTowneVineyards.com

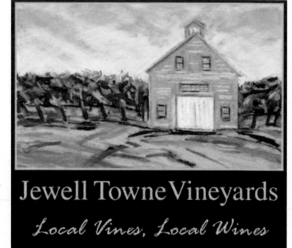

Welcome to Jewell Towne Vineyards! We are New Hampshire's oldest winery and vineyard located in South Hampton, New Hampshire on the border of Amesbury, Massachusetts and have been producing premium red, white and rosé wine since 1994. Our world-class NH made wines such as Seyval, Cayuga White. Chardonnay, Maréchal Foch, and Vidal Icewine have won acclaim from consumers and critics alike. During the past several years Jewell Towne Vineyards has truly made a name for itself in the New England wine scene by capturing more than 100 medals in international competitions due to the experience and skill of winemaker Dr. Peter Oldak.

In 1977, Dr. Peter D. Oldak, an emergency physician and his wife, Brenda, moved to a 12 acre farm in South Hampton, New Hampshire. In 1982, merely as a hobbyist home gardener, he planted six individual grape vines. Four years later, he started making wine. Each year more vines and varieties were planted to see which would do best in our climate, soil, and location, and which

varieties would make excellent quality wine in the chilly climes of the Northeast. By 1990 there were over 60 varieties of American, European, and French Hybrid grapes in the ground and it was becoming evident that the vineyard, with its southward facing slopes on the Powwow River, possessed the ideal micro-climate for wine growing. Through extensive study, trial and error, and availing himself to the best professionals in the East, Dr Oldak learned grape growing and wine making. With this knowledge, the quality of the grapes improved with each harvest and as a result of hard work, skill, and dedication, so did the wine!

At the winery you can learn about the winemaking process from vine to bottle on our guided tours, and then stay for a complimentary wine tasting to discover the premium wines that are made from New Hampshire grown grapes. The winery offers a wine cellar, a bottling room, and a spacious rustic post and beam tasting room. After you're tasting, take a stroll through our vineyard, or take time to visit the our second floor balcony which showcases an art gallery, featuring the works of noted local artists and artisans and then purchase some of our delicious and acclaimed New Hampshire made wine. We're a small, family owned craft winery and attribute our success to being local, down to earth, and by offering a wonderful experience for friends and family with an interest in any facet of winemaking. If you're coming to Jewell Towne, plan to relax and enjoy, we offer a non-intimidating environment for wine newbie and aficionado alike!

Cayuga White –
Off-dry, with hints of tropical fruit and melon.
NV- Best of New Hampshire, 2006 'Big E' Wine Competition; NV – Silver Metal, 2006 "Indy" Wine Competition

Riesling –
Floral nose, with hints of lime and orange.
NV – Bronze Medal, 2007 "Indy" wine Competition

Traminette –
Floral nose, a rich bouquet of tangerine, rose and lychee aromas.
NV- Best of New Hampshire, 2007 'Big E' Wine Competition; NV- Gold Medal, 2007 'Big E' Wine Competition; NV – Bronze Metal, 2007 "Indy" wine Competition

South Hampton White 2006 –
Semi-sweet, with rich grapefruit and Muscat flavors.
Bronze Metal, 2007 'Big E' Wine Competition

Alden 2005 –
Off-dry rosé with hints of lychee, and oak. Floral bouquet.
Silver Metal, Indiana State Fair

Maréchal Foch 2005 Private Reserve –
Full bodied, with red raspberry aromas, leather, spice and black pepper.
Bronze Metal, 2007 'Big E' Wine Competition

Zinfully Sweet Zinfandel –
A sweet, late harvest, red wine made from Zinfandel grapes. Intense flavors of blackberry and red currant.
NV – Bronze Metal, 2006 'Big E' Wine Competition

Port –
An intense red berry aroma with hints of coconut, chocolate and vanilla.

Rhapsody In Blue (Vidal Icewine) –
Nectar of the gods dessert wine.
NV – Bronze Metal, 2006 'Big E' Wine Competition

Vidal Ice Wine 2006 –
Delicious sweet dessert wine with hints of honey and apricot.
Bronze Medal, 2007 "Indy" wine Competition

LaBelle Winery

LaBelle Winery
100 Chestnut Hill Road*
Amherst, NH 03031
(603) 828-2923
www.LaBelleWineryNH.com

LaBelle Winery is situated atop Chestnut Hill in Amherst, New Hampshire. (*We do not have retail hours, our tastings and tours are by appointment only. Please contact us for more information.) We set out to make a wine that is enjoyable – that brings together family and friends around a table to revive the spirit of community. We also hope to demystify the winemaking process through educational opportunities, both hands on and through seminars, in the winter months at the winery.

Our wines reflect the orchard spirit and are made with apples and other fruits, grown in New Hampshire. The fruits are picked at their peak and then pressed and fermented the same day, resulting in an exceptionally fresh, balanced wine. While fermenting at very low temperatures to retain the fruity qualities, we paid close attention to our acid and residual sugar balance. The results: fresh, crisp, fruity wine that is easy to drink and enjoy with friends and family. LaBelle Wines are bottled unfiltered to preserve the natural fruit essence, body and flavor; a small deposit of sediment may be visible after prolonged aging. We would love to share our passion for winemaking with you! Drop us a note or stop by if you would like to learn more!

Amy LaBelle has been a corporate attorney for 12 years in Boston, Massachusetts and Merrimack, New Hampshire, but her lifelong interest in wine lead her to open LaBelle Winery to pursue her passion for winemaking. Amy is attracted to a more agrarian lifestyle and the elegance of making excellent wine. Amy makes each and every bottle of wine produced at the winery, and has slowly seen her dream realized: to make the best wine she can make with locally grown fruit and to produce a wine that will bring together family and friends to enjoy. LaBelle wines are elegant, enjoyable, easy drinking wines, made with the best and brightest local produce. Each bottle is filled with Amy's love for the ancient art of winemaking. Amy lives in Amherst, New Hampshire with her husband, Cesar, who assists in the winemaking effort and manages operations at the winery, and their son, Jackson Alejandro. Amy is grateful for the support of her family and her many friends who encouraged her to realize her dream and who help around the winery every chance they get!

Dry Apple –
Crisp Fresh Light. Small batches of our favorite apple varieties from Alyson's Orchard are fermented immediately after pressing at a low temperature. This preserves the fruity freshness, yet lends a crisp calvados nose to our flagship wine. A wonderful aperitif, this wine is also excellent with light meals or to balance a creamy, heavy one.

Heirloom Apple –
Robust Fruity Floral. Inspired by Homer Dunn, the manager at Alyson's Orchard, this unique wine is made with only our celebrated heirloom apples. Their historically valued characteristics yield a more complex wine, replete with floral notes of roses and tulips. This wine is excellent as an aperitif, with a light meal, and superb with turkey and ham.

Granite State Apple –
Crisp Subtly Sweet Fruity. Apples and maple syrup are popular co-stars in the New England food basket. In this specialty wine we add a touch of locally produced maple syrup to our fresh apple wine made from select, slow-fermented Alyson's Orchard apples. Serve this delicacy at room temperature or slightly chilled to compliment dessert or a cheese course.

Jalepeno Wine –
Spicy Fresh Bold. Made from local jalapeño peppers, this wine is excellent in salsas, marinades, dips, guacamole, dressings, fajitas and especially good as a vodka substitute a Bloody Mary! This wine is very hot and spicy so drink at your own risk!

Seyval Blanc –
Elegant Delicate Refined. In this elegant, fruity wine, we slow-fermented grapes from Alyson's Orchard, resulting in a delicate and beautiful wine, replete with floral, fruity notes and soft tannins. Excellent as an aperitif or with a light meal, this is a perfect wine to drink on a warm summer evening.

Piscassic Pond Winery, LLC

Piscassic Pond Winery, LLC
38 Oaklands Road*
Newfields, NH 03856
(603) 778-0108
www.NHMead.com
www.Piscassic.com

Here at the Piscassic Pond Winery, LLC we specialize in the unusual. Making honey wine (Mead), which most people have never heard of, puts us into a very exclusive club known mostly to home brewers and reenactors.

It all started in 2002 when the decision was made to start making Mead for resale and not just as a hobby. The owner and wine maker, Nathan Smith, had been making semi-dry honey wines for 10+ years before deciding to expand into a commercial facility. We received our licenses early in 2003 which allowed us to start making our first batch of Mead. It was ready to sell in 2004. In the following year we started introducing other flavors as well as some sweeter varieties. Now, after 4 years, we have wines that range from semi-dry to semi-sweet. We have traditional Meads as well as Melomels (Mead made with fruit) and Metheglins (Mead with herbs or spices). As of this writing, we have 3 Traditional Meads and 5 flavored options. Small batches are always in the works to test out new ideas, and new flavors are definitely on the way. *We are currently open by appointment only but plan on opening a tasting room sometime in 2009.

We purchase our honey from medium to large apiaries in New Hampshire exclusively. The apiaries we work with do a lot of orchard and field pollination. They take their bees from place to place in NH and the bees collect nectar from any flower within 2 miles of the hive location. Being able to move the bees from place to place is important to be able to keep that many bees fed. That's one of the reasons why we don't keep our own bees or extract our own honey; that kind of an operation is a full-time job in and of itself.

The Winery is named after the Piscassic Ice Pond which is pictured on the original label. This Pond was an important source of ice for refrigeration in the Newmarket/Stratham area in the late 1800's and into the early 1900's, until electric refrigerators replaced the need for iceboxes and block ice.

Honey wine is one of the oldest drinks known to mankind. It was very popular in areas that traditionally didn't grow grapes (though many of these areas are able to grow grapes now). It was also very popular in America from colonization to the Civil War.

Most of the large, commercial Meaderies produce a honey wine that is very sweet; more like a cordial than a table wine. These are more of a Celtic style of Mead. Our Mead is more like the style found in the northern areas of Europe, hence the Icelandic names. These honey wines were on the dryer side and therefore more reasonable for a table wine.

Drier   *Sweeter*

To help consumers who are unfamiliar with honey wines as well as to illustrate the difference between 3 seemingly identical Traditional Honey Wines, we've put a sweetness gauge on the labels. It's not easy to remember which name goes with what sweetness. It's a lot easier to look at the side of the bottle to compare them.

The process of making a honey wine is very similar to the process of making a white grape wine with some exceptions. Honey is so sugar-dense that the yeast cannot act on it in its natural state so the first step is to add water to it to dilute it down to about 22% sugar (which is about the same as white grape juice). At this concentration it can start fermentation and is treated like a white grape wine. The yeast is 95% done converting sugar to alcohol in 6 weeks; it's wine, but it's not good wine. At this point the wine is racked (the clear liquid is separated from the sediment at the bottom of the tank) and aged for another 9 months - that's 3 times longer than a typical white grape wine! We could sell it earlier, but the flavor is so much better with the additional time that we chose to age it for the extra time it needs.

The shorter aging time does give a grape winery an advantage, but we have some advantages that we think offset the drawbacks. We don't have to make our wine around the harvest of the fruit. Because honey is shelf-stabile we have a lot of flexibility. We can (and do) purchase honey year-round and it's ready for us when we're ready for it.

Another advantage is how we infuse the flavors. We age our wines in their most basic state: our driest Traditional Honey Wine. When we're ready we can choose to bottle it the way it is (Þurrt), add fruits and/or spices (Melomels and Metheglins), or add more honey to make them sweeter (Léttsætt, and Hálfsætt). If a grape winery runs out a particular varietal wine it may be 12 months for them to have it again. We can have some varieties replenished in as little as 2 weeks.

Honey wine has a very different mouth feel than a grape wine. It's very soft and doesn't give you the somewhat characteristic bite you get from a grape wine. Many people believe this bite comes from the alcohol and we frequently get asked if our wine contains alcohol. It does – 10 to 11.5%.

I never liked the idea of having to 'acquire a taste' for something. We have many customers that wanted to like wine but never found one that they liked. We feel you shouldn't have to make yourself like anything you don't want to. You should drink what you like, whatever that may be, but before you give up on wine give honey wine a chance. There's a reason it's called the Nectar of the Gods.

Zorvino Vineyards

Zorvino Vineyards
226 Main Street
Sandown, NH 03873
(603) 887-8463
www.Zorvino.com

Zorvino Vineyards is a small piece of Tuscany located in Sandown, New Hampshire. Our picturesque winery is located on 80 beautiful acres in the middle of a New England hardwood forest. We are committed to producing quality wines from local New England grapes carefully tended on our property, as well as interesting varietals from grapes grown in premier winemaking regions of the world, including Tuscany, Chile and Northern California. We also produce excellent fruit wines.

We are not just a winery but a destination, with a beautiful rustic post and beam manor house where we can accommodate events of all types and sizes. We have a wonderful terrace with soon to be flowing ponds and waterfalls where you can relax and have a glass of wine while overlooking our vineyards. Come sample our wines in the Zorvino Tasting Room or spend a day enjoying our Tuscan Villa in the New England countryside!

The dream of a winery began in 2001 when Jim Zanello returned from the "old country" with fond memories and wonderful stories to tell of his experiences in Italy. It was the winery visits that had captured his imagination. The quality of food, wine and life in general contrasted sharply with our typical American values and daily pace. Jim decided then to bring a taste of Europe and culture to Sandown, New Hampshire. At Zorvino Vineyards, we hope to bring good food, good wine and a chance for all to reflect on a better quality of life.

Zorvino
VINEYARDS
Baby Bluez
Blueberry Wine
Enjoy Yourself · Life Is too Short !!

Baby Bluez -
Our limited production Semi-Sweet Blueberry wine is now for sale. The aroma has wonderful blueberry tones with a touch of apricot in the background. The wine itself has a full fruit flavor with an interesting tartness on the finish that is due to its mouthwatering acidity. A great wine with spicy foods but excellent by itself as well. Very limited production of only 16 cases!

Lambrusco -
A specialty at Zorvino, our Lambrusco is a light, fruity wine yet finishes up on the dry side. We have flown our grapes in from Italy where we have secured only the freshest product available. This wine is excellent for the Summer barbeque, light enough to handle grilled chicken yet heavy enough for a pork roast.

Rosso -
We are excited to announce our very first release from our own grapes planted here in Sandown, New Hampshire! Our Zorvino Rosso is a blend of Valiant and Niagara grapes harvested in 2006 and aged a year in our stainless steel tanks in the winery. This is an easy drinking wine, medium bodied and very fruit forward. The perfect wine for full flavored or spicy foods. VERY limited production of only 7 cases....Get it while you can!

Pinot Grigio -
Crisp and medium bodied, our Pinot Grigio was made from grapes sourced from California. This white wine has wonderful apple and fruit notes, yet closes with mellow mineral tones in its pleasant finish. I'm proud to say this wine is much rounder and has more body than many of the typical sharp Italian Pinot Grigios. The perfect wine for salads and summer sipping!

Peachez 'n Cream -
Our Peach wine came out beyond our expectations! The perfect Summer sipper, this light, slightly fruity offering is like a cool breeze. Tropical fruit flavors dominate but are followed with a pleasant off dry finish. This will go great with seafood or light chicken dishes but it might be at its best all by itself.....and you WILL want another glass!

Sangiovese -
Another Tuscan specialty at Zorvino, our Sangiovese is a full-bodied and robust red wine. Utilizing select grapes from Italian growers in California, we have crafted a round, fruit forward, yet soft and silky expression of what we consider the premier varietal in Italy. Superb with pastas, pizzas and meat sauces but complex enough to stand up to steak.

Razzberry Delight -
Another of our new limited production wines, the Semi-Sweet Raspberry is a Summer treat. The aroma is all about raspberries and the taste is as if you had just eaten a bowl of fresh berries! Once again we have created a luscious fruit wine that has a dry finish which allows it to pair wonderfully with a wide range of foods. Another limited release with only 32 cases made!

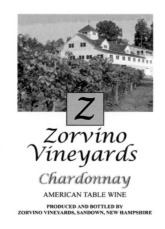

Zorvino Vineyards
Chardonnay
AMERICAN TABLE WINE
PRODUCED AND BOTTLED BY
ZORVINO VINEYARDS, SANDOWN, NEW HAMPSHIRE

Chardonnay -
This new Chardonnay is sourced from the one of the best Chardonnay growing areas of the world, California. We have created a very easy to drink style of white wine with no oak whatsoever, so all you taste is the round Chardonnay grape. Flavors of tropical fruit dominate the palate. This unoaked Chardonnay is excellent with seafood of any type or chicken dishes.

Rhode Island

Diamond Hill Vineyards

Diamond Hill Vineyards
3145 Diamond Hill Rd.
Cumberland, RI 02804
(800) 752-2505 or (401) 333-2751
www.FavorLabel.com

Diamond Hill Vineyards has been growing fine wine grapes since 1976. We produce Estate Pinot Noir, Pinot Noir Blanc, River Valley White, Blackstone Blush, Cranberry Apple, Spiced Apple, Peach and Blueberry wine. We specialize in Custom or Personalized labels for our wines, especially in our Favor Line, Holidays and labels for any occasion.

Our hours: Tasting room and gift shop, Thursday thru Saturday, noon to 5:00 pm. Office, Tuesday thru Saturday, 9:00am to 5:00pm. Holiday hours (November thru Christmas: Tasting room and gift shop, Tuesday thru Sunday, noon to 5pm. Office, Tuesday thru Saturday, 9:00am to 5:00pm.

The Berntson family planted their first vines in 1976. Planting has continued and 4 acres of the noble grape Pinot Noir is now growing. Peaches are also being grown. Because fine Pinot Noir requires long aging, the Berntsons decided to revive the old New England tradition of making wine from New England fruits such as apples, cranberries, peaches and blueberries. The tradition has been updated using modern equipment and techniques. The complex and delicious wines that result are rapidly becoming true New England classics.

The 220 year old vineyard house is situated in 34 acres of beautiful surroundings. In the Gift Shop you will find an assortment of gift baskets and Rhode Island specialty items. Also check out our extensive line of designer labels for all occasions at the tasting room. The front lawn is available for events and occasions such as wedding ceremonies, photo opportunities, bridal and baby showers, anniversary parties, etc. Up to 60 people can be accommodated under our tent and gazebo.

Blueberry Wine –

The Maine Wild Blueberries are ideal to make a richly fruity and sweetly balanced port style. We ferment this with special yeast to create an alcohol content of up to 14%. This is especially good with complex cheeses. Limited quantity, please inquire for availability.

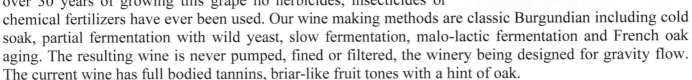

Berntson Pinot Noir –

Red wine from the noble Pinot Noir grape is the 2004 vintage. In over 30 years of growing this grape no herbicides, insecticides or chemical fertilizers have ever been used. Our wine making methods are classic Burgundian including cold soak, partial fermentation with wild yeast, slow fermentation, malo-lactic fermentation and French oak aging. The resulting wine is never pumped, fined or filtered, the winery being designed for gravity flow. The current wine has full bodied tannins, briar-like fruit tones with a hint of oak.

River Valley White –

This white wine is from purchased fruit and sometimes blended with Riesling or other white wine juice (predominately a chardonnay blend.) Slightly off dry with a popular fruity finish. The river referred to is the Blackstone River, named for the first settler (1635) in what is now Cumberland RI, where our vineyard is located. The river valley is now a National Historic Corridor.

Blackstone Blush –

A chardonnay blended with merlot. This blush wine is slightly sweet with merlot top notes, a good choice with lighter fare. Named in honor of Rev. William Blackstone, first English settler of what is now Boston and Cumberland RI.

Cranberry-Apple Wine –

A blend of New England's favorite seasonal fruit, 25% cranberries and 75% apple wine, together make a sweet-tart wine perfect for festive occasions like Thanksgiving and Christmas. We have a large selection of Holiday Wine Labels that can also be customized to you or your company's specifications using logos, photos or other art work.

Spiced Apple Wine –

The fall, holiday and winter season favorite. A blend of apple wine and spices that include cinnamon, cloves, Valencia orange peel and other traditional spices from Davidson's. Sweet enough for mulling as is or add some honey to taste.
RECIPE: 1 bottle Spiced Apple Wine, 4-5 tbs. light brown sugar, 1/2 cup apple juice or cider (optional). Heat in saucepan. Do not boil.

Peach Wine –

After Dinner dessert treat. A unique wine, intensely peachy and frankly sweet to balance the natural acidy of whole, fresh peaches. Serve with chocolate anything!

Sparkling Cider –

Used for a non-alcoholic special occasion. Sparkling "Champagne" cider is the perfect alternative to real champagne. We can custom label this to make your Holiday or "Thank You" gift so special.

Raspberry Wine –

Pure raspberry flavors, penetrating tart/sweet finish. Limited availabilty, please inquire.

Greenvale Vineyards

Greenvale Vineyards
582 Wapping Road
Portsmouth, RI 02871
(401) 847-3777
www.Greenvale.com

Welcome to Greenvale Vineyards located along the beautiful Sakonnet River in Portsmouth, Rhode Island, five miles north of downtown Newport. Greenvale is a farm that has been in the same family since 1863. It is listed on the State and National Registers of Historic Places. Our goal is to maintain this cultural resource, a piece of American history in a productive and meaningful way. Beautiful grapes, delicious estate grown wines and the creation of a wonderful destination for visitors is our path to this goal.

Greenvale produces small quantities of exceptional estate grown wines. The terroir, the environment in which the grapes are grown and the wine produced, produces wonderful delicious award winning wines. You can clearly taste what makes Aquidneck Island such a supreme place to farm. Come tour the vineyards, taste and learn about delicious wines, enjoy the beautiful tasting room, the lovely views of the vineyards and the river and hear about a piece of cultural history.

Cortlandt Parker, the farm's fourth generation, and his wife Nancy Parker started to grow grapes here as a hobby in the 1960's. In the early 1980's, the Parker's realized the pressure that farm land would experience and decided to embark on the development of a commercial Vineyard to develop a viable farming operation. Greenvale started its grape growing operation as growers for Sakonnet Vineyards across the river in Little Compton. In the early 1990's, the Parker's with the assistance of their daughter Nancy Parker Wilson and her husband William Wilson embarked on the development of Greenvale's own wine. A consultant that they had hired from the North Fork of Rhode Island believed that their fruit was too good and should make a wine under its own Greenvale label. Today we produce about 3,500 cases of wine annually from our 24 acres of grapes

In 2000, under the leadership of son in law William Wilson, a Boston architect, Greenvale restored the Stable which allowed Greenvale to be open for tours and tastings and to develop a popular music series. Please join us for Jazz on Saturdays from Memorial Day though October. Come to one of our book signings by local National authors throughout the year, or attend a Friday night concert featuring Blues, Irish and Folk Music. Our Stable turned Tasting Room provides a wonderful venue for our entertainment. The Tasting Room has great acoustics and is an award winning restoration for Adaptive reuse. It is also a wonderful place for your own special event, wedding, rehearsal dinner – the list goes on. Greenvale Vineyards is open for Vineyard Tours and Wine Tastings from 10:00 am to 5:00 pm Monday through Saturday and 12:00 pm to 5:00 pm on Sunday.

ROSECLIFF PINOT GRIS – The Pinot Gris grape has proven to grow beautifully on Aquidneck Island. This wine has lovely aromas, delicate fruit flavors, is soft on the palate and has a very pleasant finish. Excellent with lighter meals, such as grilled seafood or summer salads. 480 cases produced.

2004 GREENVALE CHARDONNAY – A well balanced wine, our 2004 Chardonnay is a dry, light wine with soft fruity aromas. The wine has delicate fruit flavors, characteristic of a cool climate chardonnay grape, and a pleasing finish. The 2004 is delicious by itself or with mild or light foods. 40% barrel fermented and aged, 60% stainless steel. 230 cases produced.

2005 CHARDONNAY SELECT – The 2005 Select has aromas of oak on the nose. Nicely balanced, the Select is aged for 9 months in 100% French oak barrels which gives this Chardonnay a pleasant acidity and smooth, lingering finish. A great pairing with an entrée such as lobster or chicken off the grill. The Select is produced primarily from the oldest of our chardonnay grape vines, which were planted in 1983. 113 cases produced.

2006 VIDAL BLANC – This grape is a wonderful French/American hybrid that produces an extremely aromatic and pleasantly flavored wine. It is a delicious, bright wine, especially good with ham, salads, cheeses, and spicy foods. Medium dry. Fermented in stainless steel. 660 cases produced.

SKIPPING STONE WHITE – Skipping Stone is a blend of Cayuga and Vidal Blanc. Very light in color, the wine is aromatic, with a bright, crisp, floral nose; delicious and refreshing on the palate. It is slightly off dry, with a nice balance of fruit and acidity. This wine is great by itself, with cheese, or a simple meal, and is also sensational with spicy foods. Fermented in stainless steel. 970 cases produced.

2004 CABERNET FRANC – Our Cabernet Franc is a well balanced, medium bodied, Bordeaux style red. The complex aromas of plum and earth, with soft tannin in the finish, make this an excellent wine to pair with almost any meal; especially with grilled or roasted meats. 80% Cabernet Franc, 20% Merlot. Barrel aged. Approximately 170 cases produced.

THE ELMS MERITAGE – Rhyming with "heritage," this 2003 vintage is a blend of Cabernet Franc, Merlot, and Malbec, three traditional varietals of Bordeaux. The wine is a medium bodied, dry red – wonderful aromas of berry, smoke, and subtle spice with a delicious, lingering finish. It is great by itself as well as with flavorful foods or dark chocolate. 56% Cabernet Franc, 33% Merlot, 11% Malbec. Barrel aged. 205 cases produced.

Charlotte Village Winery

Charlotte Village Winery
3968 Greenbush Road
Charlotte, VT 05445
(802) 425-4599
www.CharlotteVillageWinery.com

Charlotte Village Winery is located in Charlotte Vermont just south of Burlington and Shelburne Vermont. We are about five miles south of the Vermont Teddy Factory just off of Route seven. Our Vermont winery features free wine tasting from Memorial Day weekend to December 31st, from 11:00am to 5:00pm. There is a large deck where wine customers can sit and enjoy spectacular views of the Adirondacks after tasting our award winning wines.

Charlotte Village Winery, in Vermont's Champlain Valley, is a unique boutique winery. Our winery features both fruit and grape wines. The fruit wines are made from fresh Vermont fruits. Our selections include a Strawberry Resiling Wine, Raspberry Wine, a Peach Chardonnay Wine and three styles of Blueberry Wine. The grape wines include Merlot Wine, Cabernet Sauvignon Wine, Gamay Wine, and Pinot Grigio Wine. All these wines are made here in Vermont. Our grape wines are made from grapes grown in the Lodi region of California.

Charlotte Village Winery was founded in 2001 by fourth generation Vermonters, William and Colleen Pelkey and their son Will Pelkey. We started to produce blueberry wines with the blueberries from our 10 acre field in 2001. Our winery was completed in 2004 and we began producing several different types of wines. Charlotte Village Winery opened its doors to the public in July 2005. Located in Charlotte, Vermont at 3968 Greenbush Road; approximately 15 miles south of Burlington. Be sure to come for the free wine tasting to select the wines that satisfy your pallet while overlooking our blueberry fields and enjoying the views of the Adirondack Mountains from our tasting deck.

Dry Blueberry Wine - A Dry full bodied red wine with spicy overtones. Pairs well with red meats. This wine is aged in American Oak for one year. A gold metal winner from the American Wine Society.

Merlot - A medium bodied red wine, that goes well with all red meat dishes. Aged in French oak for two years. This wine won a silver medal from Tasters Guild.

Pinot Grigo - This is a dry white wine produced by Charlotte Village Winery with grapes from the Lodi region of California. It has a particularly nice bouquet and goes well with fish and white meat dishes.

Cabernet Sauvignon - A Charlotte Village Winery Cabernet Sauvignon is handcrafted by forth generation Vermonters and made with hand selected grapes from California. This medium bodied red wine is aged in French Oak and will add flavor and zest to any red meat meal.

Semi Dry Blueberry Wine - American Wine Society Award Winner Not overly sweet but just enough to, bring out the wine's blueberry flavor. Good with red meats, and also with scallops. Aged in American oak for 8 to 10 months. A silver medal winner.

Gamay - Made in our winery with grapes from the Lodi region of California. It is a light semi-dry red wine. It goes well with traditional wine dishes that are on the light side, such as sandwiches, burgers, pizza, shrimp, and scallops.

Sweet Blueberry Wine - A blueberry wine made with enough sweetness to be a desert wine. This wine goes well with any desert but especially with cheesecake, drizzie a little of the wine on top. Serve chilled.

Sweet Raspberry Wine - This wine is made with 100% fresh Raspberries. This wine can be used as a picnic wine, after dinner wine or serve with a strong cheese. Enjoy with a group of friends. A gold metal winner with geat aroma and strong Raspberry flavor. Serve chillrd.

Sweet Strawberry Blush Wine - Fresh strawberry wine blended with 40% Reisling white wine. This strawberry wine has a soft strawberry nose with a slight tart finish. A very nice sipping wine. Serve chilled.

Flag Hill Farm

Flag Hill Farm
PO Box 31
Vershire, VT 05079
(802) 685-7724
www.FlagHillFarm.com

Here at Flag Hill, we handcraft traditional, farmhouse-style Vermont Hard Cyders. Vermont Hard Cyder is made by hand on an organic, 250-acre hilltop, family farm with lovely panoramic views of the Green Mountains. At Flag Hill, founders Sabra Ewing and Sebastian Lousada have planted acres of orchards with more than 80 old and new varieties of cider apples. Pure and natural, unsprayed apples are the only ingredient in their artisanal Vermont Hard Cyder. Sebastian began making traditional country wines in England when he was 12. He now oversees the entire wine making process, managing the winery and the orchards, where the cider apples used to make all of Flag Hill Farms unique products are nurtured. Sabra, the founder of VerShare, a community organization dedicated to improving life in the small town of Vershire Vermont, has deep roots in sustainable rural living. Sabra manages Flag Hill Farm's Sales and Marketing and networks with retailers and restaurateurs throughout Vermont. When you're traveling or vacationing here in beautiful Vermont, why not call ahead and add Flag Hill Farm to your itinerary? We'd be glad to show you around, give you a tasting, and you can even buy some Vermont Hard Cyder to take home! We hope to see you soon.

About "Vermont Hard Cyder"

Amanda Hesser, writing in the New York Times, calls hard cider, "a drink that can be more graceful than wine." In a 2001 article, she wrote, "In the past decade, cider making has revived, with a small cluster of fruit growers around the country turning to cider with a winemaker's approach - some are like fragrant, delicate Champagnes, others bracing, yeasty brews." Here at Flag Hill Farm in the Green Mountains of rural Vermont, we take this same slow, traditional, wine-making approach to our own hard cyder.

We make two varieties of prize-winning hard cyder, Sparkling and Still, in small batches, right here on our family farm. To distinguish our handmade, farmhouse product from apple cider and mass-market carbonated apple 'wines,' we call our product, Cyder with a "y."

We grow and harvest many of the apple varieties used in our hard cyder, and buy only certified organic local, unsprayed and wild apples from neighboring farms. Flag Hill Farm Hard Cyder is bottled in limited release and is available only in Vermont! We are truly excited about introducing our dry, crisp Vermont Hard Cyders as a sophisticated new beverage alternative for good cooks, food lovers, and wine connoisseurs throughout New England. We think they're delicious, and hope you agree.

Vermont Still Hard Cyder

Dry, crisp, and complex. A mellow, country-style table wine. All natural. Made from wild and cultivated, unsprayed, Vermont-grown, tart cider apples. Our Hard Cyder is made by hand in the traditional, old ways, with no additives, sulfites, or any artificial ingredients. Aged two years, in the barrel. Blended from a mix of varietal ciders. Excellent for cooking. 8½ % alcohol; no sulfites, Organic.

Vermont Sparkling Hard Cyder

Sparkling and dry. Never fruity or sweet. Our Sparkling Hard Cyder makes a festive addition to any party and is the perfect compliment to fine foods and desserts. Hand crafted in The Old French Champagne Style or "Methode Champenoise," our cyder is transformed from a dry still wine to a magnificent sparkling elixir. Aged two years before bottling; then aged for another year in a handsome Champagne bottle and finished with an authentic champagne cork and wire hood. Excellent tiny bubbles. 9½ % alcohol; no sulfites, Organic.

F.H.F Distillery introduces two certified organic dry, fruit brandies to the local artisanal hard drink scene: Stair's Pear an American 'Poire William' and Pomme de Vie, the first apple brandy produced in Vermont since prohibition! We think of these crystal clear 'eaux de vies'as "the spirited essence of fruit." They provide the perfect complement for regional and seasonal cooking, and a stylish & unique after dinner digestif or apres-ski drink! Look for both in Vermont liquor stores now.

"Stair's Pear"

Certified organic pears from the oldest farm in Vermont. Double distilled from local Bartlett Pears. 80 proof in a pretty tall clear flute. Organic.

"Pomme-de-Vie"

Pomme de vie is inspired by the French apple brandy, Calvados. Also known as an 'eau-de-vie' or 'water of life,' our Vermont apple brandy is a smooth, dry, and crystal clear distillation of the essential flavor and aroma of apples. Made with traditional, time-honored techniques, from our own unsprayed apples in dozens of varieties. We double distill our slow-fermented and barrel-aged hard cyder over an open flame to produce a brandy with maximum flavor and aromatics. Use in any recipe calling for apple brandy or Calvados to create unique and special Vermont entrees and desserts that will be long remembered! 80 proof, Organic.

Flag Hill Farm Vermont Hard Cyder took "Best Dry Cider" at Ginger Brook Farms Cider Tasting, 2000. When challenged by 26 ciders, including domestic, English commercial, and Vermont farmstead ciders, we won hands down! Flag Hill Farm Vermont Hard Cyder is featured in a new Williams-Sonoma cookbook, "New England / New American Cooking," by Molly Stevens. Available at Williams-Sonoma stores. Boston Magazine featured Flag Hill Farm Cyder in the Wine section of the October 2007 issue, "their Flag Hill sparkling cider is a mouthwatering yeasty, dry version that puts most American sparkling wines to shame…" Members of Vermont Fresh Network, in the coming months look for postings of seasonal, recipes using Hard Cyder and/or our Brandy with local ingredients, all perfectly suited to slow, country-style, home cooking at www.VermontFresh.net. We also hold frequent tastings at fairs, food coops, and other events. We are available to schedule a tasting at your business location in Vermont. Contact us for information today!

Grand View Winery

Grand View Winery
Max Gray Rd
East Calais, VT 05650
(802) 456-7012
www.GrandViewWinery.com

Grand View Winery is a family operation. Phil, the wine maker, began dabbling in wines for fun 30 years ago. In 1996 he started the winery in our barn. Two years later we acquired the house next door and moved the production and retail there. The following year we opened a retail/tasting room at the Cold Hollow Cider Mill. It's open year round.

Most of the fruits are grown at the winery or purchased locally. We focus on fruits that grow easily in Vermont. Our fruit wines are not overly sweet. Limiting the sweetness brings out more of the natural flavors of the specific fruit. All wines are aged at least a year with the red grape two years. We use no oak barrels or oak chips to avoid masking the true flavors.

Come off the beaten path. Enjoy our rural setting with 50 mile views. Bring a lunch to enjoy with a selected wine sitting outside soaking up the views, flower gardens, and tranquility. Tour the winery and learn about wine making and taste the award winning results.

EXPERIENCE THE ORIGINAL VERMONT, journey along back country winding through fields and farms unchanged for the last century. At the end of your trip, experience the tranquil setting of Grand View Winery. Flowery gardens and a gallery of Vermont artists provides a wonderful background for some delightful tasting. Tour the wine making learning center and see for yourself the process that turns grapes and simple fruits into distinctive wines.

In the Stowe area? Stop by our retail/tasting room at the Cold Hollow Cider Mill Complex, Rte 100, Waterbury Center.

Rhubarb
Organically raised rhubarb. A delightful dry white wine. "Close to a Pinot Grigio"

Foch ("Foe-sh")
A red wine from French Hybrid Mareshal Foch grape. No oaking to bring out the flavor of the grape. Low tannin, light bodied.Great red for those who prefer whites, Great summer red. A dry wine.

Seyval
A white wine from the French Hybrid Seyval grape, light, dryish, full of fruit flavor along the lines of a German wine. Major national award winner in 1999 (Awarded by the American Wine Society with only 8 wineries receiving recognition in New England).

Riesling
Classic style, lightly sweet and very smooth. Nuances of peach and apricot give it a fruity flavor. A real treat.

Montmorency Cherry
Semi-dry with a pleasant balance of a light sweetness and the tartness of the cherry.

Pear wine
Just pears for a fresh pear bouquet. Lightly sweet. Great with Brie.

Blueberry Apple
A blend of blueberry and apple for a sweeter wine. Similar to a White Zin in sweetness. Served cold, with or after dinner.

Dandelion Wine
From the dandelion blossoms comes a very different white wine very aromatic. Very Limited quantity. Lightly sweet.

Raspberry Infusion
A combination of red raspberry and red grape for a unique semi-dry wine ideal for sipping, after dinner or instead of a dessert. Take a moment to fully enjoy the raspberry bouquet.

Blueberry Wine
Organic Blueberries full of flavor reminiscent of a Beaujolais. Great with chicken or after dinner. Lightly sweet.

Elderberry Wine
Deep, rich and complex sweeter wine. Ideal for after dinner or with dessert. Matches exceptionally well with a very sharp cheddar.

Mac Jack Hard Cider
All apple, 5% alcohol, only a slight touch of sweet and lightly carbonated. A refreshing change.

North River Winery

North River Winery
201 VT Rte. 112 River Road
Jacksonville, VT 05342
(800) 585-7779 or (802) 368-7557
www.NorthRiverWinery.com

The North River Winery, Vermont bonded winery #1, is located in the picturesque foothills of Windham County, situated along the North River, a popular trout fishing stream, in the small village of Jacksonville, Vermont. The 1850's farm house and barn, which house the winery, are filled with the charm of an age when wines were made by local residents.

Started in 1985 the winery has gone from making 2,500 gallons of wine annually to about 20,00gallons. Approximately 90% of the fruit used by the winery is grown at the Dwight Miller Orchards in Windham County, a State of Vermont, certified organic Orchard. We make 11 different wines, ranging from a very dry, varietal wine, Vermont Pear to sweeter dessert-style wines such as Vermont Harvest, which contains cinnamon and Vermont maple syrup. We also make a Rhubarb wine, which is 100% organic and does not contain any sulfites! Although fruit wines can be made sweet they can also be made into dry dinner wines that are not much different from dry grape wines.

All fermentation, bottling and distribution are done on the premises. We produce about 100,000 bottles of wine each year. Approximately 60% of that is sold at the winery's retail locations. We have a distributor in Vermont servicing our retail customers and restaurants.

The Winery operates a seasonal tasting room at the Hogback Mountain Gift Shop located on Route 9 in Marlboro, Vermont from late May through October. Our year-round tasting room is located in Bennington, at the Camelot Village on Route 9 West in Bennington and is open seven days a week from 10:00am to 5:30pm. There is also a tasting room at the winery, which is open daily from 10:00 to 5:00.

The North River Winery's location in Southern Vermont makes it an enjoyable day trip from almost anywhere in New England. Described as "A MUST SEE" by Yankee Magazine, especially during foliage season! The Winery is open daily from 10:00am to 5:00pm for FREE tastings and sales. We offer free tours late May through December. Other hours by appointment. Group packages are available. All areas of the Winery are handicapped accessible.

For over 15 years the wines produced by North River Winery have been consistent award winners in the annual, International Eastern Wine Competition held in Walkins Glen, NY. The 2000 competition resulted in 3 medal winners, Woodstock White, Autumn Harvest and Vermont Harvest. In addition, the Winery entered the Indiana International Wine Competition, held annually at the Indiana State Fair. This competition resulted in 8 medals, 8 selections were presented for competition! Silver: Woodstock White, Woodstock Red, Autumn Harvest and Vermont Harvest. Bronze: Cranberry Apple, Raspberry Apple and Midnight Gold. The Vermont Harvest was a gold medal winner in 1999!

Our Dinner & Dessert Wines:

Vermont Pear - Uses 100% Vermont-grown Bartlett Pears, bone dry and smooth with a delicate pear bouquet. A superb dinner wine.

Green Mountain Apple - Semi-dry with a refreshing crisp green apple tartness. Excellent with seafood, especially scallops or shrimp.

Northern Spy - This dry, oak-aged apple wine is crisp with a chardonnay-like quality. An exquisite dinner wine; great with pasta primavera.

Vermont Blush - A dry wine with a hint of raspberry in the finish. Excellent choice where a white wine is appropriate; fish, chicken or pork.

Woodland Red - A dry light-bodied red wine that is excellent with red meat, tomato dishes and pizza. Add a little to your homemade tomato sauce for a great taste experience.

Metcalfe's Hard Cider - A Gold Medal Winner at the International Eastern Wine Competition, semi-dry thirst quencher. Bring along on your next picnic.

Rhubarb - A predictably tart, semi-dry, medium bodied wine that is just delightful. This wine contains no sulfites and the rhubarb is 100% organically grown.

Cranberry Apple - Tart, semi-dry, a seasonal favorite that accompanies turkey and game dishes.

Raspberry Apple - Semi-sweet, slightly tart, full of fresh raspberry in the bouquet and flavor, great by itself or in a spritzer.

Blueberry Apple - Sweet, full bodied, with a distinct blueberry flavor. Serve with dessert or by itself. Drizzle over vanilla ice cream for a unique taste experience.

Vermont Harvest - Our best seller! Reminiscent of a sweet sherry, made with apples, cinnamon and 10% Vermont Maple Syrup. Great chilled or heated.

Ottauquechee Valley Winery

Ottauquechee Valley Winery
5573 Woodstock Rd. (Rt. 4)
Quechee, VT 05059
(802) 295-9463
www.NorthRiverWinery.com

In September of 1999 we opened the Ottauquechee Valley Winery. The "Quechee Winery" is located on Rte. 4 in the historic Quechee Gorge Village complex in Quechee, Vermont. Just East of the famous Quechee Bridge and Gorge, a famous attraction in the Upper Valley Region.

In 1875, the Woodstock Railroad Company built a bridge (an engineering feat of its day) to span the Quechee Gorge, Vermont's most spectacular natural wonder. For over 50 years, the train traveled back and forth between White River Junction and Woodstock, Vermont carrying visitors and local folk, grain, bags of wool, bolts of fabric, lumber, tools, grain -- commodities for the Upper Valley and far beyond.

Progress eventually brought the automobile, resulting in the train's final run in 1933. The rail bed was converted to highway use and, today, is Vermont's only direct east/west roadway.

Each year thousands of vacationers visit the small Village of Quechee, Vermont, to view the spectacular Quechee Gorge, shop are numerous area stores, and dine at local restaurants. One of the most popular destinations for shopping is our very own Ottauquechee Valley Winery store, located just east of the famous Quechee Bridge and Gorge in the "big red barn" in the historic Quechee Gorge Village complex on Rte. 4. The "Quechee Winery" is filled with Vermont made wines, Cabot specialty cheeses, gourmet olive oils and an eclectic selection of wine related items. We're open everyday, 10:00 to 5:00, and of course FREE wine tastings will be provided. Groups are welcome, but please call or email us first to make a reservation. This way we can make sure we can be adequately staffed for a large group of guests.

Our Dinner & Dessert Wines:

Vermont Pear - Uses 100% Vermont-grown Bartlett Pears, bone dry and smooth with a delicate pear bouquet. A superb dinner wine.

Midnight Gold - Made from locally organically grown rhubarb lightly sweetened with a touch of Vermont honey. It is especially appropriate with desserts.

Autumn Harvest - This semi-sweet wine is made from a blend of Vermont apples and Montmorency cherries is lightly tart. It has a distinct cherry pie aroma and taste. Serve chilled for a special treat, try it warmed up with mulled spices.

Woodstock Red - A lightly oaked semi-sweet wine made from a blend of low brush wild blueberries and Vermont grown apples. Being light-bodied and fruity, it is excellent with beef and tomato dishes.

Vermont Apple - Semi-dry with a refreshing crisp green apple tartness. Excellent with seafood, especially scallops or shrimp.

Woodstock White - A lightly oaked dry wine made from a blend of Vermont grown Northern Spy apples and Vermont pears. Being light-bodied, this wine is superb with fish shellfish or poultry.

Snow Farm Vineyard

Snow Farm Vineyard
190 West Shore Road
South Hero, VT 05486
(802) 372-9463
www.SnowFarm.com

We're Snow Farm Vineyard. What you'll see at the vineyard began as a dream and a passion in 1995 – the fierce desire to keep land agricultural in Vermont. With land becoming more valuable for its development potential than for its worth farming, we were concerned with the future of our state, afraid of losing what makes Vermont unique. Fortunately, our dream also became the dream of others, and together, Vermont's first commercial grape vineyard and winery came into existence in 1996. It is our hope that we can provide an alternative for farmers, so that they can rededicate their land to a new agricultural pursuit and keep it working rather than selling it for residential or commercial purposes.

We are open from 10;00 to 5:00 daily from May 1 through December 31. Self-guided vineyard tours are available at all time during the business hours. Tastings are available at all times during business hours. Tastings and tours are free for individuals. Group tours and after-hours events need to be scheduled in advance. And, yes, we do weddings. Off-season, please call; we are around. Besides wine, we also have wine accessories and Vermont specialty products, including Vermont specialty foods that pair with our wines.

We're Molly and Harrison

We're often asked if we are the owners. Actually, the bank is the owner, but they're letting us play here for the next twenty years or so. I guess, technically, we are the proprietors, but this venture would not exist but for our investors. We chose the name "Snow Farm" because both elements of the name symbolized the essence of Vermont. Besides, Ernest and Julio Lebowitz didn't quite work.

2005 Estate Seyval Blanc – Nice delicate aromas. Orange nose and citrus notes. Well balanced and very versatile for pairing purposes.

2006 Estate Seyval Blanc – Partially fermented and aged in oak with delicate wood flavors leading to an extremely well rounded wine. Compares to a light Chardonnay.

2006 American Riesling – A dry to off-dry Riesling with delicate grapefruit characteristics. Crisp and clean. Pairs beautifully with light seafood. An excellent wine.

Snow White – 2006 Estate Wine. A nice, sweet blend of Cayuga and Seyval. Enjoy with appetizers, cheese or relaxing with seven friends.

2005 American Leon Millot – Lively red fruit accentuates this non-oaked, dry wine.

2006 Estate Leon Millot – Rich, ripe red fruit with oak, yet smooth texture. Pairs well with most foods or stands alone.

2006 Estate Baco Noir – Both berry and Montmorency cherry in the nose and on the palate. Pinot Noir in color. Pairs well with red meats.

2006 Estate Pinot Noir (very limited) – Ruby red color with fresh berry tones, especially current. Soft tannins. Perfect balance. An excellent aging wine. Pairs well with tenderloin with sautéed mushrooms.

Rose Red – 2005. How do we ask you to enjoy Snow White's sister without seeming offensive? A delightfully fruity, sweeter red wine that can be enjoyed at room temperature or chilled, like a Sangria. Pairs with Spanish or Mexican.

2006 Estate Vignoles – Late Harvest. We're all over the map on this one. Some of us taste peach, almond, and honey, others pears and orange zest, and still others taste pineapple and butterscotch. Regardless, it's a great dessert wine!

2005 Estate Vignoles – Late Harvest. A sauterne-style late harvest wine made with over 80% botryis (Noble) rot. Marmalade, honey and apricot nose and palate.

2006 Estate Vidal Blanc Ice Wine – A very special wine with lots of exotic fruit, like mango and pineapple, and leechee nuts. Nice honey on the palate too. Best served chilled after dinner. Another excellent vintage.

Apple Dessert Wine – A late harvest ice wine style. Sweet and rich in intense apple flavors. Made for after dinner enjoyment or for that special occasion.

Index